Mission:

Possible

Finding and Fulfilling Your Life's Assignment

Gregory Lan Ijiwola

CityLight Publications

Chicago, IL

Mission: Possible
Finding And Fulfilling Your Life's Assignment
ISBN: 0-9746735-4-4
ISBN 13: 978-0-9746735-4-7
Copyright © 2011 by Gregory Lan Ijiwola

Published by
CityLight Publications
P.O Box 15478
Chicago, IL 60615
www.thecitylight.org

Cover design by GodKulture, LLC.

CONTENTS

DEDICATION

To Pastor Kayode Ijisesan,

You helped me to better define my mission, kick-starting it

To Pastor Sam Adeyemi,

You came in and preserved it when it would have faltered in a new phase.

To Pastor Sunday Adelaja,

You keep showing me its unrealized possibilities.

To Debo, my sweetheart, I appreciate your partnership.

To Jesse, Joshua and Pearl, arrows in my quiver.

May you find your missions early in life and may they exceed mine in every good way.

FOREWORD

Perhaps the most urgent and pressing need of today`s church is for the ordinary believer to discover how he can add value to himself and to the Kingdom of God. Too many people are just busy going to church. Yet, unaware of the awesome opportunity and privilege they have in serving God.

Probably, one of the most frequent questions that I get asked is "How do I discover my calling?" Well, if that is your question then this book is for you. Pastor Lan has done an excellent job by presenting us with a book that answers these questions.

This book is written for the ordinary believer and unbelievers as well. The book has been so clearly and carefully written to ensure that every single reader gets the message of the book. Moreover, this is not just a book that helps you to discover your calling, it goes beyond that, it gives you the instruments that will establish and ground you in the things of God.

Additionally, I make bold to say that there aren't many people in the church today that have a thorough grasp of this Kingdom truth and understanding the way Pastor Lan does, therefore, the most valued piece of this book for me is the way that the Gospel of the Kingdom has been so thoroughly presented. So, for all who desire to be used as God`s instrument in advancing the Kingdom of God, this book is a must-read!

Thank you so very much, Pastor Lan. You have done a great job for the body of Christ, and I am very proud of you. And as the popular maxim goes, "More grease to your elbows!"

Pastor Sunday Adelaja,

Senior Pastor, Embassy of God Church,

Kiev, Ukraine.

ACKNOWLEDGEMENTS

This book would not have been possible without the help of certain individuals. Thanks to Efe Adefulu and Osen Imoukhuede who transcribed my teachings at the CityLight Leading Lights Training. I also appreciate Emi Aprekuma and the rest of my editorial team at CityLight Publications for their excellent work. Your dedication and flexibility has made this mission possible.

Thanks to my wife, Debo for overseeing the entire project. You're the best!

INTRODUCTION

My journey of purpose began at the age of 16, while reading a book titled, *The Seven Great Prayer Warriors* by Collin Whittaker. The book tells the story of seven individuals that were greatly used of God in their generations: George Muller, Hudson Taylor, Praying Hyde, Charles Finney, David Brainerd, Rees Howells, and Madame Guyon.

While reading this book, I had an encounter with God that indelibly marked my young mind and set the course of my life. I heard God speaking to my heart that I was to devote my life to service in the ministry of preaching and teaching. The voice I heard was so clear that it was as if someone was with me in the room that I was.

At first, I ran from this call because I had other ideas of what I wanted to do with my life. It wasn't fun. I finally surrendered to God a couple of years later, and since that time till now, twenty years later, I have been on a journey pursuing that call. I have either pastored, taught or been involved in some sort of evangelistic ministry initiative or church planting work almost without interruptions throughout this period, including during my college years.

Finding the assignment of God for my life (at least the broad outlines of it) at a very early age is something I am extremely grateful to God for because it helped me avoid wasting years pursuing other less important things.

Currently, I pastor The CityLight Church, a church we planted six years ago in Chicago. In my pastoral work here and in other churches, some of the most common questions people often ask is: How can I know God's purpose for my life? or, How can I find out what He has called me to do? In addition, those who seem to know what they are called to do want to know how to step out and start pursuing it.

This book is an answer to these questions. It lays out, in a simple way, the process of discovering your assignment in life and progressively pursuing it. The goal is to transform you from a spectator into an active participant in the exciting things God is doing in your generation, enabling you to lay aside every encumbrance and jump into the race that God set for you.

Follow me as we press towards your glorious destiny in life and get ready to leave behind a life of boredom and drudgery. Read prayerfully; then, study the scriptural references. Afterwards, apply them to your life. Finally, take action on what you discover. I believe God that this book will be a life-changing encounter for you. Pray the following prayer before we begin.

Dear Lord, as I read the following pages, open my eyes of understanding that I may see Your glorious truth concerning my calling in life. Let me encounter Your Spirit as I read. Let me see with clarity your plans for my life and be empowered to pursue my high calling in Christ. Thank you Lord! In Jesus' Name.

CHAPTER 1

GOD'S ASSIGNMENT FOR YOUR LIFE

"Before I formed you in the womb I knew you; Before you were born I sanctified you; I ordained you a prophet to the nations." (Jeremiah 1:5)

According to the U.S department of Health and Human Services, a main commonality between suicidal people is a feeling that their lives lack purpose. This sense of futility and hopelessness is said to be a leading characteristic found in people who attempt suicide. This grim fact is an evidence of the toll of purposelessness in our days. Rarely do people who are pursuing their life missions take their own lives. In contrast, they are usually resilient, hopeful and energized about life. Knowing your mission in life is essential.

Take a walk down the aisles of your local electronic store. Every product has a manufacturer's name and a description of what it was manufactured to do, usually accompanied by a manual of how it functions. Some are essentials necessary for life. While others allow us to comfortably carry out our daily lives. Others are simply for our recreational purposes. All of them, though, were created to solve a particular problem. That is, each of them has a unique purpose.

Now, take a look at nature. Is there anything you see in nature without a particular purpose? The sun sustains life on earth. Soil provides nutrients and a stable place that enhances plant growth. Plants release oxygen and provide food.

You are not an exception. Just like all the products in a store and all the elements of nature have a purpose, there is a predetermined reason for your existence. You are not just a product of random chance in an unpredictable universe. There was a purpose in the mind of your creator before He ordained your life on the earth. Your life has meaning. Everything God creates, adds value to the rest of God's creation and advances certain intents in God's heart. Before you were ever born, you were an idea living in the mind of God. Don't take my word for it. Look at what the Bible says:

"Your eyes saw my unformed body. All the days ordained for me were written in your book before one of them came to be. (Psalm 139:16)

"Listen to me, you islands; hear this you distant nations; Before I was born the Lord called me; from my birth He has made mention of my name." (Isaiah 49:1)

Before anything was formed, you were in Him. He knew you. You were an intent in His mind. In fact, the purpose of your existence on earth is to carry out that intent. Therefore, you are a person on a mission— someone with an assignment. When this life is over, you will return to your commissioner, God, to give an account of your missionary endeavor on the earth.

This knowledge—that your life is not meaningless—makes life exciting! You can stop simply existing and truly start to live. Escape being part of the statistics of those slain by the epidemic of meaningless living and respond to the call of God.

THE CALL OF GOD

The call of God is the specific summon from God to accept or execute God's will on earth. Discovering your call, accepting it and progressively answering it, is the process of living a purposeful life. The Bible speaks of several dimensions of God's call. It primarily speaks of God's call to salvation.

This is the first call humans have to experience and answer before stepping into other dimensions of His call. The call to salvation is the act of God's grace in which a person is summoned by God from sin and alienation and given a new life in Christ and the hope of eternal life.

This call is not based on any merit or work of the human, but solely on the grace of God.

"...who has saved us and called us with a holy calling, not according to our works, but according to His own purpose and grace which was given to us in Christ Jesus before time began." (2 Timothy 1:9)

God must first call, or invite us to enter into a relationship with Him. He does this by opening our minds to our need to repent and accept Christ into our lives. Jesus said:

"No one can come to Me unless the Father who sent Me draws him; and I will raise him up at the last day." (John 6:44)

The "draw" mentioned in the verse of scripture is God's invitation to salvation. Salvation is the state of being free from the power of death. From this freedom comes the knowledge that you are God's child and the power to access the inheritance that comes with being a child of God.

Many who have received this invitation from God have not responded. If you have accepted Christ into your life, then you have accepted that invitation, and by grace, you are now a child of God, a heir of salvation, heaven-bound and a partaker of the benefits of redemption.

The calling of God to salvation is a glorious call. It is a calling out of darkness into God's marvelous light. It is a call to be a part of God's holy nation, His peculiar people and His chosen generation. It is a call to be part of His royal kingdom of priests. It is a great privilege.

But you are a chosen generation, a royal priesthood, a holy nation, His own special people, that you may proclaim the praises of Him who called you out of darkness into His marvelous light; (1 Peter 2:9)

However, the call to salvation is not the only call of God the Bible speaks about. There are other summons of God that we are to heed after we are saved. For instance, 1 Thessalonians 4:7 speaks about our call to holiness.

"For God did not call us to uncleanness, but in holiness."

And 1 Corinthians 1:9, speaks of our calling into fellowship with Christ.

> *"God is faithful, by whom you were called into the fellowship of His Son, Jesus Christ our Lord."*

THE CALL TO MINISTRY

Though the call of God to salvation is vital because it necessarily precedes the call to ministry, our focus in this book is your call to ministry. This call refers to God's summon that you carry out a certain assignment for Him during your earthly life. This is your call to service; your missionary assignment on earth.

We see many examples in scriptures of people being called by God to unique assignments.

Noah was called to build an ark to preserve life on earth;

Abraham was called out of his father's house to begin a new family of God in a new land;

7

Moses was called to deliver the people from Pharaoh's bondage and lead the people of God to the Promised Land;

Aaron was called to be a priest of God;

Joshua was called to lead the people to conquer the Promised Land and divide it among the people of Israel;

Deborah as a judge was called to deliver Israel from the Philistines;

Nehemiah and Ezra were called to take a role in the rebuilding of the broken walls and the temple of Jerusalem;

Esther was called to preserve the people of God using her position as a queen;

John the Baptist was called to be a forerunner of the Savior

The twelve apostles were called in various ways to use all they learned from Jesus to witness about

His resurrection and serve as founders of the church; and

Paul was called to preach the gospel to the Gentiles.

These are just some of the unique appointments God gave in the scriptures. Notice that these calls extend across the genders and diverse backgrounds and delve into several fields, including military, political and humanitarian assignments.

From the moment each of these individuals discovered their assignments and proceeded to start carrying them out, they became people of purpose and destiny.

The call to ministry extends beyond the people referenced in scriptures. Everyday, God is still calling people to a plethora of assignments.

WHAT IS MINISTRY?

"Ministry" is a word that has been abused in the body of Christ. It is used to refer to many things that it is not. It is therefore important to properly define the word. First, it will be helpful to identify what it is not. Ministry is not a title or position. It is not limited to a function within a church.

Also, it is not an organization or association. It is also not synonymous with preaching. It is also not the exclusive preserve of some. It is not an exclusive club that only a few privileged ones such as pastors and evangelists can patronize.

Rather, ministry extends to every saved person. It is the divine call to fulfill a specific assignment. Ministry is a function or a task handed down by God to a person for which he or she must give account for. It is simultaneously the execution of God's purpose for your life.

Because ministry is a result of God's compassion for humanity, this purpose is not restricted to tasks within the church, but covers every area of human need. Everywhere humanity hurts, God has a ministry designed for it, an assignment to heal it and a person He has predestined to carry out this assignment. Ultimately, ministry is *God's hands touching human needs through the instrumentality of a yielded person.*

Therefore, ministry is stewardship. That is, one who submits to ministry is a messenger, an errand-person for God; he or she is a conduit through which God flows and touches a block of humanity.

If you have heeded the call of God to salvation, you have been called to one form of ministry or the other. Paul says:

"For by grace you have been saved through faith, and that not of yourselves; it is the gift of God, not of works, lest anyone should boast. For we are His workmanship, created in Christ Jesus for good works, which God

prepared beforehand that we should walk in them.

(Ephesians 2:8-10)

You were saved by grace, not by your works. After you were saved, however, you were called to do some good works. These works are the assignment that God predetermined for you. This means that there is a call you must answer and a ministry you must fulfill.

You are God's workmanship, His work of art, designed specifically to fulfill that ministry. It is when you are fulfilling that calling that you are at your best. It is then that you are in your element. It is within your calling that you hit the high notes of fulfillment in life.

Your calling is that urge that places a necessity on you and makes you cry out like Paul, "Woe is me if I preach not the gospel!" Your assignment is the divine impulse that compels you to leave other things and act in a certain way - The athlete just wants to run. The writer must write. The preacher feels the "preach". It is the "teach" in the teacher, the "lead" in the leader and the "sing" in the singer.

When this impulse intersects with a divine instruction from God and a human necessity on the earth, it is called ministry—the outworking of God's grace from one human toward another in a segment of the earth realm.

THE KINGDOM ASSIGNMENT

When God created the earth, His intention was to create a place that would be a replica of heaven—an extension of God's domain. Every segment of the earth was supposed to be covered with the knowledge of the glory of the Lord. So, God created Adam and Eve and gave them the assignment of filling everywhere with His kingdom.

The word, kingdom simply means the "king's domain or dominion." The kingdom is the extent of the authority, power and rule of a king. Adam was to have dominion, fill the earth and subdue it with the glory of God.

But that wasn't what happened. Instead, Adam and Eve sinned, falling short of the glory of God. The kingdom on earth was lost. The spheres of the earth became subject to Adam's new Lord, Satan, who began filling the earth with his kingdom.

As a consequence, the curse replaced the blessing. This curse, Satan's influence, began to operate in the family, business, government, economic, entertainment and other arenas of the earth. Satan became the god of the world system and dominated the lost children of God and their environment.

But thank God the story did not end there. God, in the person of Jesus Christ, came into the world and took that authority back from Satan, giving it to the church in His name. Jesus then gave us the same assignment, in the Great Commission, of taking His kingdom to the whole earth by preaching and living the gospel. That is, Jesus sent us to reclaim the gates of the enemy to our world and to fill those places with the message, character and power of the kingdom.

When speaking of taking the kingdom to the segments of the earth. I do not in any way refer to establishing a theocracy or establishing a dictatorship over people. I also do not advocate a violent or forceful conversion to Christianity. Rather, "establishing the kingdom" is about spreading the compassion, wisdom, righteousness, peace and joy of God everywhere.

As we proclaim the gospel to others and live exemplary lives of godliness, we should be establishing systems based on the principles of God's word and thus, inspiring people to praise God.

"But you are a chosen generation, a royal priesthood, a holy nation, His own special people, that you may proclaim the praises of Him who called you out of darkness into His marvelous light;" (1 Peter 2:9)

MINISTRY IN THE SEVEN SPHERES

In recent times, the segments or spheres of the world to which believers have been called to fulfill their assignments have been categorized into seven. Loren Cunnigham, in his book, *Making Jesus Lord* wrote:

> Sometimes God does something dramatic to get our attention. That's what happened to me in 1975. My family and I were enjoying the peace and quiet of a borrowed cabin in the Colorado Rockies. I was stretched out on a lounge chair in the midday warmth, praying and thinking. I was considering how we Christians – not just the mission I was part of, but all of us – could turn the world around for Jesus.

> A list came to my mind: categories of society which I believed we should focus on in order to turn nations around to God. I wrote them down and stuck the paper in my pocket.

> The next day, I met with a dear brother, the leader of Campus Crusade For Christ, Dr. Bill Bright. He shared with me something God had given him – several areas to concentrate on to turn the nations back to God! They

were the same areas with different wordings here and there that were written on the paper in my pocket. I took it out and showed Bill and we shook our heads in amazement. Here's a list (refined and clarified a bit over the years) that God gave me that sunny day in Colorado:

1. The home

2. The church

3. Schools

4. Government and politics

5. The media

6. Arts, entertainment and sports

7. Commerce, science and technology

These seven spheres of influence will help us shape societies for Christ.[1]

What Cunningham and Bright saw here was simply the arena the Great Commission was intended to play out by the Lord Jesus when He said:

Go therefore and make disciples of all the nations,
baptizing them in the name of the Father and of the Son
and of the Holy Spirit, (Matthew 28:19)

And He said to them, "Go into all the world and preach
the gospel to every creature. (Mark 16:15)

The Eleven were commissioned and empowered after becoming disciples to go and teach all nations (*ethnos*), to go into all the world (*kosmos*) and to preach the gospel to every creature (*ktisis*).

"All the nations" and "world" here has traditionally been interpreted in geographical terms. So we would send missionaries to nations like India or China to fulfill the Great Commission. However, a deeper look at the words reveals that there are other ways in which they could be defined. Jesus certainly wasn't restricting the preaching of the gospel to geographical divisions alone. He was also speaking of cultures, spheres, people groupings and segments of the earth.

For ease of remembrance, these seven spheres have been categorized and rendered in alphabetical form as follows:

A: Arts, entertainment, and sports

B: Business, commerce and finance

C: Church and Religion

D: Distribution and Media

E. Education, science and technology

F: Family and Home

G: Government, politics and law

SPHERE MISSIONARIES

We are very familiar with ministry in the church and religion sphere. Pastors and other clergy minister in and from this sphere. This sphere includes the pulpit ministry. However, only a very small portion of the body of Christ is called to this sphere. The majority are called to the other six spheres.

One of the ways we have erred is the emphasizing of ministry in one sphere at the expense of the other spheres. However, God is bringing an awakening. Many believers are beginning to see that to take the gospel to the world; callings must be fulfilled outside the church walls. Marketplace ministers, anointed professionals, politicians, business people, scientists, parents, social workers, athletes, educators and a host of creative professionals in the arts and entertainment are all essential. This has been God's intention all along.

Your purpose in life is to work out an assignment from God, to extend His kingdom and meet a particular need of humanity in one or more of these spheres. First, you will have to discover to which sphere(s) God has called you. In the next chapter, we will focus on the discovery of your assignment.

CHAPTER 2

DISCOVERING YOUR ASSIGNMENT

"...Eye has not seen, nor ear heard, Nor have entered into the heart of man The things which God has prepared for those who love Him. But God has revealed them to us through His Spirit..."(I Corinthians 2:9, 10)

The Apostle Paul once sent a message to Archippus. "And say to Archippus," Paul wrote, "Take heed to the ministry which you have received in the Lord, that you may fulfill it." (Colossians 4:17)

In this reminder, Paul charges Archippus to ensure that he carries out the assignment he had received from God. Here, we see three important truths about callings. First, callings are received from the Lord. Second, callings require the cooperation of the one who is called. And, third, callings can either be fulfilled or remain unfulfilled.

The first truth deals with discovery. It makes it clear that ministry is not something that any human can conjure. You do not design or choose your calling. Rather, you discover it and then cooperate with God in order to fulfill it. Humans may confirm the calling of God on you, but they do not confer this purpose to you. We see this truth exemplified in the following passage:

As they ministered to the Lord and fasted, the Holy Spirit said, "Now separate to Me Barnabas and Saul for the work to which I have called them." (Acts 13:2)

The Holy Spirit makes clear that the work for which Barnabas and Saul were being separated for was one that the Holy Spirit had ordained.

Another passage also emphasizes this truth. As it is said of Aaron speaking about the calling to be high priest, the scriptures say, "no man takes this honor on himself but he that is called." (Hebrews 5:4). Thus, true ministry is not a product of your family's persuasion. Likewise, your purpose cannot solely be determined by your pastor's impression or your spouse's preference.

Finally, your calling is not simply your preference. It is not a product of your speculation and is not originated in your feelings or desires. Any desires that lead to your calling must be God-inspired.

Rick Warren, speaking of purpose in his book, *The Purpose-Driven Life* says, since your purpose in life is not a product of research or speculation, the calling of God for you can only then be discovered through the understanding of the working of God in your heart.[2] God has not left you in the dark concerning his call for you, but he has put certain pointers to it in your makeup and in his word. He hid it in you.

Scripture makes a similar point, *"But as it is written, Eye hath not seen, nor ear heard, neither have entered into the heart of man, the things which God hath prepared for them that love him." (1 Corinthians 2:9)*

To protect you, the plan of God for your life is a mystery, a hidden secret. He hid it *for you* not *from you*, in the same way the bank will hide your money for you, so that an intruder will not have access to what belongs to you. This hidden treasure can then be withdrawn when you provide certain agreed upon secret passwords and identifying documents.

One of God's avenues for unveiling this secret is revelation, a divine disclosure of hidden truth. Paul, speaking of how he discovered his calling said it was given to him by revelation.

"If indeed you have heard of the dispensation of the grace of God which was given to me for you, how that by revelation He made known to me the mystery (as I have briefly written already, (Ephesians 3:2, 3)

Paul's calling was dramatic.

"So I said, 'Who are You, Lord?' And He said, 'I am Jesus, whom you are persecuting. But rise and stand on your feet; for I have appeared to you for this purpose, to make

you a minister and a witness both of the things which you have seen and of the things which I will yet reveal to you. I will deliver you from the Jewish people, as well as from the Gentiles, to whom I now send you, to open their eyes, in order to turn them from darkness to light, and from the power of Satan to God, that they may receive forgiveness of sins and an inheritance among those who are sanctified by faith in Me.' "Therefore, King Agrippa, I was not disobedient to the heavenly vision," (Acts 26:15-19)

Thus, through a life changing vision of the Lord Jesus, Paul realizes he was mistaken in his calling. He was not called to destroy Christianity, but rather to spread it.

Not everyone who receives a call from God has a sensational experience like Paul did. For most, the communication of the call is usually unspectacular, coming as a natural result of their persistent fellowship with God. This would be the testimony of Peter, who was summoned by Jesus to become a fisher of men from his fishing business.

Hudson Taylor, the missionary to China, also received a simple call. After reading a gospel tract, Taylor's eyes were opened to the gospel; he became certain that he was called to spread the gospel to the almost closed empire of China. He wrote of how he discovered his call in his autobiography:

> Not many months after my conversion, having a leisure afternoon, I retired to my own chamber to spend it largely in communion with God. Well do I remember that occasion? How in the gladness of my heart I poured out my soul before God; and again and again confessing my grateful love to Him who had done everything for me — who had saved me when I had given up all hope and even desire for salvation —
>
> I besought Him to give me some work to do for Him, as an outlet for love and gratitude; some self-denying service, no matter what it might be, however trying or however trivial; something with which He would be pleased, and that I might do for Him who had done so much for me.

Well do I remember, as in unreserved consecration I put myself, my life, my friends, my all, upon the altar, the deep solemnity that came over my soul with the assurance that my offering was accepted. The presence of God became unutterably real and blessed; and though but a child under sixteen, I remember stretching myself on the ground, and lying there silent before Him with unspeakable awe and unspeakable joy.

For what service I was accepted I knew not; but a deep consciousness that I was no longer my own took possession of me, which has never since been effaced. It has been a very practical consciousness.

Two or three years later propositions of an unusually favorable nature were made to me with regard to medical study, on the condition of my becoming apprenticed to the medical man who was my friend and teacher. But I felt I dared not accept any binding engagement such as was suggested. I was not my own to give myself away; for I knew not when or how He whose alone I was, and for whose disposal I felt I must ever keep myself free, might call for service. Within a few months of this time of consecration the impression was wrought into my soul that it was in China the Lord wanted me.[3]

An important lesson from Hudson Taylor's experience is that he discovered his calling as an overflow of his communion with God. It is still that way. The discovery of calling is what is called vision or revelation.

Vision is like pregnancy—it is a product of intimacy. As you develop intimacy with the Spirit of God through worship, prayer and meditating on God's word, the womb of your spirit is impregnated with the vision of God for your life. It begins to live and grow in you in preparation for its delivery. As you spend time in the presence of God, He begins to infuse in you His own heart, His passion and burden for a certain segment of His creation.

PRIMARY PURPOSE

Though your calling is discovered through a life of communion with God, this communion is actually your primary purpose. You were created to bring pleasure to God. You were made to know Him and fellowship with Him. That's why you were made in His image.

It takes beings of the same class to truly fellowship together. God made you in such a way that you can talk to Him and He to you. You can commune with Him and enjoy each other's presence. It is out of this fellowship, the fulfillment of your primary purpose, that His assignment for your life, your secondary purpose, is revealed.

PRIESTS AND KINGS

Every believer was made a priest and a king. The scripture explains this point saying:

"And from Jesus Christ, the faithful witness, the firstborn from the dead, and the ruler over the kings of the earth. To Him who loved us and washed us from our sins in His own blood, and has made us kings and priests to His God

and Father, to Him be glory and dominion forever and ever. Amen. (Revelation 1:5, 6)

This passage speaks of two aspects of our calling on the earth—our kingly ministry and our priestly ministry. The kingly ministry is our ministry to our fellow humans. In our kingly ministry, we bring about the expression of the kingdom of God through our involvement in human earthly affairs.

The other aspect is our priestly ministry—our ministry to God. It encompasses our vertical relationship with the Father. Our priestly ministry is our spiritual connection with God in prayer, fellowship and worship. Peter discussed the priesthood ministry, writing:

"You also, as living stones, are being built up a spiritual house, a holy priesthood, to offer up spiritual sacrifices acceptable to God through Jesus Christ." (1 Peter 2:5)

God made you in such a way that you can truly communicate with Him, responding to His conversation with you. It is out of this fellowship, the fulfillment of your priestly ministry, that His assignment for your life, your kingly ministry, is revealed

Accordingly, our priestly calling is a priority. The kingly ministry feeds off the vitality of our priestly ministry. Ultimately, our spiritual connection with Him determines the manifestation of His presence and effectiveness in our earthly relationships.

Look at the example of Adam. He was made in the image of God. God would come in the cool of the day to fellowship with him. From that fellowship, God gave him his assignment of taking care of the garden. His fellowship with God led to the discovery of his calling.

There is a garden you are to tend to, a portion of the earth which you were created to manage. If you too will fellowship with the Lord constantly, He will reveal to you the section of the earth you were created to tend.

ACTIVITIES IN THE WOMB

Your calling is intertwined with who you are as a person. In fact, God had already determined your calling before you were formed in the womb. He told Jeremiah:

""Before I formed you in the womb I knew you; Before you were born I sanctified you; I ordained you a prophet to the nations." (Jeremiah 1:4, 5).

Paul also spoke of a pre-birth separation to a calling:

"But when it pleased God, who separated me from my mother's womb and called me through His grace, to reveal His Son in me, that I might preach Him among the Gentiles, I did not immediately confer with flesh and blood, (Galatians 1:15, 16)

It was also said of John the Baptist,

"For he will be great in the sight of the Lord, and shall drink neither wine nor strong drink. He will also be filled with the Holy Spirit, even from his mother's womb. (Luke 1:15)

"When Elizabeth heard Mary's greeting, the baby leaped in her womb, and Elizabeth was filled with the Holy Spirit."(Luke 1:41)

And of Jacob and Esau,

"The Lord said to her, "Two nations are in your womb, and two peoples from within you will be separated; one people will be stronger than the other, and the older will serve the younger" (Genesis 25:23).

To digress a little, anyone familiar with political debates in America will be aware of two opposing camps on the issue of abortion—the pro-life and pro-choice camps. The pro-life camp believes abortion is wrong because it is the murder of an innocent child and potential fully-grown human, since, to the pro-life camp, life begins at conception.

The pro-choice camp believes the choice to abort or not to abort should be left to the woman since the baby lives in her body. Many people who are pro-choice believe that abortion is wrong but would prefer the woman make the call of whether to abort or not to abort.

However, some people who are pro-choice, in defending their positions go to the extent of saying that aborting a child in the womb, especially in the early parts of the pregnancy, is not killing a human. Rather to these pro-lifers, abortion simply kills an embryo which is part of the woman's body.

But, what is God's view about life in the womb? God talked to Rebekah about the two children in her womb, calling them nations and declaring the outcome of their lives before they were born. God saw them as two humans with unique purposes and potentials. The plans for these children predated their conception. This concept of a pre-birth purpose is not isolated to one particular passage, but one that runs through the Bible's entirety.

For example, the psalmist also alluded to it:

"For you created my inmost being; you knit me together in my mother's womb. I praise you because I am fearfully and wonderfully made; your works are wonderful, I know that full well. My frame was not hidden from you when I was made in the secret place, when I was woven together in the depths of the earth. Your eyes saw my unformed body; all the days ordained for me were written in your book before one of them came to be." (Psalm 139:13-16)

You can see that lots of God-activities go on before a child is born. God knows unborn children and ordains them for a purpose. He declares how their lives should be and can fill them with His Spirit from the womb. They can sense things in the womb and react to them. God separates children in the womb for unique purposes to be fulfilled when they are born. He wonderfully creates them to the specifications of what it would take for them to fulfill their purposes.

With so much activity going on in the womb, pregnant women should be seen as destiny carriers. They are carrying the future of the world and God's plan. The future great preachers, scientists, politicians, inventors, problem solvers—people with specific answers to the problems of the world are residing now in the wombs of pregnant women.

With the termination of any of these lives, the world loses something. Let this be an encouragement to you if you are pregnant. Bless your unborn child continually. Let it be an admonition if you are considering an abortion. Don't kill that nation. Don't end that destiny. God knows more about who you have in your womb than you do. Listen to Him.

Most importantly, let it be an inspiration to you that your life is not without meaning. That you are not an accident of unprotected sex. There are no illegitimate children, only illegitimate parents. No matter the circumstances surrounding your conception, you were on His mind. You are not a nuisance. You are special in His plans. So, be the nation God created you to be.

CLUES IN YOUR MAKEUP

There are clues in your makeup that point to your calling. You were designed in such a way that fulfilling your calling is the most natural thing you can do. Your being cries out for the fulfillment of your calling. You were shaped for it. I came across the concept of SHAPE, an acronym describing the unique design of everyone for the fulfillment of their assignments, in Rick Warren's *The Purpose Drive Life*:

S - Spiritual gifts. When you became a believer, certain gifts begin to function in your life as a result of the workings of the Holy Spirit. Identifying these gifts can help you understand your place in life.

H - Heart. This has to do with your passion. Mike Murdock says, "the people that unlock your compassion are the ones you've been sent to." What you love is a pointer to what you are called to do. The problems that infuriate you are the one's you've been called to correct.

A - Abilities. These are natural talents and abilities that you possess like singing, writing etc.

P - Personality- Everyone is a combination of certain personality traits called temperaments. Some are introverts, others extroverts. God wants to express Himself through your unique personality. You don't have to become another person. You are the best you that He needs.

E - Experience - This includes family, educational and career experience. Your painful experiences are also included.[2]

Finding your SHAPE is a great exercise in understanding your unique design for influence on the earth.

STEPS TO LOCATING YOUR CALLING

Here are some steps you can take in locating your calling in life:

1. Accept Jesus Christ as your Lord and Savior and be filled with the Spirit

2. Focus on cultivating a consistent and quality life of communion with God through prayer and the bible

3. Practice a consecrated lifestyle. This is an attitude of full surrender to God regarding His plans for your life. You totally surrender all your own plans and ideas to His. You are completely willing to do whatever He desires you to do, be whoever He desires you to be and ready to go anywhere He wants you to go without any hesitation or unwillingness.

One of the ways you can develop this attitude is by sincerely praying consistently, a prayer of consecration similar to what Jesus prayed over and over in the garden of Gethsemane, "*Lord, not my will but yours be done.*"

4. Locate yourself in the word of God. There are certain general things God has spoken about you in His word.

For example, the New Testament has a lot to say about who you are in Christ. Meditating on the truth of your identity in Christ will help you find yourself. For a more in-depth study of this, see my book, Identity in Christ.

5. Be sensitive to the simple directions of the Spirit of God in you. His ministry is to guide you into all truth. He is sent to you to reveal what God has prepared for you (1 Corinthians 2:9-12). This revelation may come in different ways: an impression, a voice, a vision, a strong conviction etc.

When I received my calling from God, the voice of the Spirit came to my heart in a way that was audible to me telling me specifically that He was calling me to dedicate my life to the pulpit ministry. It doesn't have to be spectacular and it most likely will not but God knows how to get the point across to you. Just make sure you are on the look out for it. Fasting can enhance your sensitivity to the communication of God in your spirit.

6. Watch out for divine orchestrations. As you begin to seek God about your calling, God may arrange events in your life that point you toward your calling. You may meet people, find yourself in repeated circumstances that seem to be passing the same message across to you. Joseph experienced this in His own call.

God orchestrated the events of his life from his Father's house to the place in Egypt or Paul who was on his way to Damascus and unexpectedly had his calling revealed by a divine arrangement of God. David got to see Goliath without knowing about him beforehand. He was only on his way running errands for his father.

Some of the important steps you will take in life will be presented to you unexpectedly through seeming coincidences and chances encounters but know that it is the hand of God arranging these coincidences behind the scenes.

6. Get Busy. Don't be idle. Analyze your SHAPE and find a place of service in your local church that resonates with

you. Plug yourself into the work of the kingdom in this avenue. When you don't know what to do, do what you know. As you are faithful in the general, God will entrust you with the specific.

"Whatever your hand finds to do, do it with your might; for there is no work or device or knowledge or wisdom in the grave where you are going. (Ecclesiastes 9:10)

GOD CALLS BUSY PEOPLE

Have you noticed that God has a penchant for calling busy people? It is fascinating to read stories of divine encounters of men in the Bible. From the Old to the New Testament, one theme threads through all the incidents: the people God appeared to in order to give an assignment were all busy doing something before they were called. Let's look at a few of them.

Now Moses was tending the flock of Jethro his father-in-law, the priest of Midian, and he led the flock to the far side of the wilderness and came to Horeb, the mountain of God. There the angel of the Lord appeared to him in flames of fire from within a bush. Moses saw that though the bush was on fire it did not burn up. (Exodus 3:1,2)

Joseph, a young man of seventeen, was tending the flocks with his brothers...Joseph had a dream (Genesis 37:2,5).

The angel of the Lord came and sat down under the oak in Ophrah that belonged to Joash the Abiezrite, where his son Gideon was threshing wheat in a winepress to keep it from the Midianites. When the angel of the Lord appeared to Gideon, he said, "The Lord is with you, mighty warrior."
(Judges 6:11,12)

After the death of Moses the servant of the Lord, the Lord said to Joshua son of Nun, Moses' aide: "Moses my servant is dead. Now then, you and all these people, get ready to cross the Jordan River into the land I am about to give to them—to the Israelites. (Joshua 1:1,2)

Now Jesse said to his son David, "Take this ephah of roasted grain and these ten loaves of bread for your brothers and hurry to their camp. Early in the morning David left the flock in the care of a shepherd, loaded up and set out, as Jesse had directed. He reached the camp as the army was going out to its battle positions, shouting the war cry. As he was talking with them, Goliath, the Philistine champion from Gath, stepped out from his lines and shouted his usual defiance, and David heard it. (1 *Samuel 17:17-23*)

So Elijah went from there and found Elisha son of Shaphat. He was plowing with twelve yoke of oxen, and he himself was driving the twelfth pair. Elijah went up to him and threw his cloak around him. Elisha then left his oxen and ran after Elijah...He took his yoke of oxen and slaughtered them. He burned the plowing equipment to cook the meat and gave it to the people, and they ate. Then he set out to follow Elijah and became his servant. (1 *Kings 19:19-21*)

As Jesus was walking beside the Sea of Galilee, he saw two brothers, Simon called Peter and his brother Andrew. They were casting a net into the lake, for they were fishermen. "Come, follow me," Jesus said, "and I will send you out to fish for people." At once they left their nets and followed him. Going on from there, he saw two other brothers, James son of Zebedee and his brother John. They

44

were in a boat with their father Zebedee, preparing their nets. Jesus called them, and immediately they left the boat and their father and followed him. (Matthew 418-:22)

After this, Jesus went out and saw a tax collector by the name of Levi sitting at his tax booth. "Follow me," Jesus said to him, and Levi got up, left everything and followed him. (Luke 5:27-28)

Meanwhile, Saul was still breathing out murderous threats against the Lord's disciples. He went to the high priest. and asked him for letters to the synagogues in Damascus, so that if he found any there who belonged to the Way, whether men or women, he might take them as prisoners to Jerusalem. As he neared Damascus on his journey, suddenly a light from heaven flashed around him. He fell to the ground and heard a voice say to him, "Saul, Saul, why do you persecute me?" "Who are you, Lord?" Saul asked. "I am Jesus, whom you are persecuting," he replied. "Now get up and go into the city, and you will be told what you must do." (Acts 9:1-6)

Saul also met Samuel while looking for his father's donkey. All these passages testify to the fact that God places value on diligence. He doesn't recruit lazy people for His special assignments. He calls those who have their hands full trying out something, working on some natural endeavor. This is pretty logical because anyone who is faithful in natural things will transfer that same attitude to spiritual things and anyone who is tardy regarding natural things will be the same when it comes to spiritual things.

The question for you then is: is your attitude toward your job, your care for your natural possessions, and effort toward your seemingly little assignments qualifying you or disqualifying you for God's call on your life? Remember, only if you are faithful in little, will you be committed over much.

THE IMPORTANCE OF CHURCH

This need to be faithful in little underscores the importance of being part of a local church. The local church offers you the opportunity to discover your calling through the various ministry opportunities present. The church is a springboard to your calling. As you plunge yourself into the ministry of your church, you set in motion, the law of faithfulness which will lead you into your specific calling in God. In the next chapter, we will discuss the role of the local church in fulfilling your calling.

CHAPTER 3

THE CHURCH — A SPRINGBOARD

"And I also say to you that you are Peter, and on this rock I will build My church, and the gates of Hades shall not prevail against it. (Matthew 16:18)

J ust as rockets need launching pads, divers need springboards and arrows require bows, every calling needs the church for full expression. According to God's design, callings are forged, released and preserved in and through the body of Christ. The church is indispensable in your quest to fulfill your calling.

The word "church" is used in a couple of senses. A first definition is the universal church which comprises every individual who has come to trust and accept Christ as their Lord and Savior. This is the body of Christ.

Membership in this universal body transcends geography, culture, nationality or race. It is the household of faith, the people of God.

The second sense of the word refers to the local church—the local expression of the universal church. A local church is formed wherever born-again individuals come together to fellowship and worship regularly in any setting. There are all kinds of local churches. There are ethnic ones or multi-ethnic ones, denominational or nondenominational ones, house churches, work place churches etc.

Membership in the universal church is automatic. The only requirement is genuine profession of faith in the Lord Jesus Christ. However, being a part of a local church usually requires deliberate steps by the believer to locate and assimilate into a particular one.

THE NEED FOR A LOCAL CHURCH

There are some who believe that being part of the universal church is enough. There are two categories of such people. The first includes those who deliberately are not part of any local church for any reason, but depend solely on either their own personal devotional lives or television ministries for their spiritual growth.

The second category consists of those who hop from church to church without commitment to any particular local church. Both categories are precarious. God expects every member of His body to have a consistent local church where they live out their faith under the guidance and nourishment of a shepherd.

Living out of order with this divine imperative exposes you to a lot of dangers. Jesus said being without a shepherd leads to harassment and distress.

Then Jesus went about all the cities and villages, teaching in their synagogues, preaching the gospel of the kingdom, and healing every sickness and every disease among the people. But when He saw the multitudes, He was moved with compassion for them, because they were weary and scattered, like sheep having no shepherd. Then He said to

His disciples, "The harvest truly is plentiful, but the laborers are few. Therefore pray the Lord of the harvest to send out laborers into His harvest."(Matthew 9:35-38)

Your calling will not be fulfilled in isolation but in a company. Your calling is nurtured in a two-fold manner—generally as a member of the body of Christ and specifically as a member of your local church. Therefore, there is a local church you are meant to be a part of, where you can grow and contribute to the increase of the body of Christ.

"But, speaking the truth in love, may grow up in all things into Him who is the head—Christ—from whom the whole body, joined and knit together by what every joint supplies, according to the effective working by which every part does its share, causes growth of the body for the edifying of itself in love." (Ephesians 4:15-16)

You will be unable to walk in the fullness of your calling if you hop from church to church, or refuse to be part of a church. Joining a church on the internet or on TV is not enough. You must physically engage in a local church if you have the freedom in your nation to do so. Being part of a church is essential for the following reasons:

A. Fellowship and Partnership

You are a member of the body. Every organ in a body needs other organs to survive and carry out its role. A church provides opportunities for fellowship with like-minded believers. You will have a pool of partners that you can join to mutually support one another in the fulfillment of your callings. Your family will also have a place they could call their spiritual home and develop godly relationships.

"So now you Gentiles are no longer strangers and foreigners. You are citizens along with all of God's holy people. You are members of God's family." (Ephesians 2:19, NLT)

B. Support and Covering

Every calling of God will be opposed by Satan, so in carrying out your assignment, you will face challenges and opposition. At times, you will even be tempted to quit. It is during those tough times that your positioning in a church provides a covering for you. Your church will provide you with brothers and sisters that can pray for and with you, counsel you, stand with you and encourage you on. You will have shepherds who watch over your life and feed you with knowledge and wisdom.

"And being let go, they went to their own companions and reported all that the chief priests and elders had said to them. So when they heard that, they raised their voice to God with one accord and said: "Lord, You are God, who made heaven and earth and the sea, and all that is in them"(Acts 4:23,24)

C. Equipping

Being part of a local church also exposes you to the ministry gifts of the pastors, teachers, prophets, evangelists and apostles. These ministry offices were set in the church by Jesus, the head of the church, for the purpose of equipping believers for the work of the ministry. In other words, your church has been specifically gifted by God to help you find and fulfill your calling.

"And He Himself gave some to be apostles, some prophets, some evangelists, and some pastors and teachers, for the equipping of the saints for the work of ministry, for the edifying of the body of Christ" (Ephesians 4:11)

These offices are set in the church to mobilize and train the saints for the carrying out of the work of the ministry. In other words, these offices are anointed to provide a platform through which the callings of the saints can be realized.

The Role of Pastors

There is a direct connection between fulfilling your ministry and the role of the offices mentioned here, including the office of a pastor. This is because the local church is a flock led by a shepherd. As a member of a local church, you will enjoy the privilege of being shepherded by a pastor. This is God's design. This is one of the benefits of being part of a local church. Your pastor is anointed to help you realize your calling.

Pastors are also instructed by God to feed, instruct and maintain watch over the sheep of God in the local church. Paul admonished the elders of the Ephesian church:

Therefore take heed to yourselves and to all the flock, among which the Holy Spirit has made you overseers, to shepherd the church of God which He purchased with His own blood. *(Acts 20:28)*

The scripture also explains the response church members are to display towards the shepherd's leadership.

Obey those who rule over you, and be submissive, for they watch out for your souls, as those who must give account.

Let them do so with joy and not with grief, for that would
be unprofitable for you. (Hebrews 13:17).

D. Corporate Anointing

As a consistent member of a local church, the anointing that is effectively working in your life multiplies. When believers fellowship together, each brings the specific anointing of God on them. These specific giftings are combined, forming a more complete expression of God's grace. This is what is called the corporate anointing.

The corporate anointing comes into manifestation when more than one believer is in the same place and there is a singleness of purpose between them. The Scriptures indicate that not only is this somewhat different from the individual anointing—in the sense that it affects more than one person –but also that the corporate anointing seems to be one of greater power than simply the sum of the individuals' power.

"When the Day of Pentecost had fully come, they were all with one accord in one place. And suddenly there came a sound from heaven, as of a rushing mighty wind, and it filled the whole house where they were sitting. Then there appeared to them divided tongues, as of fire, and one sat upon each of them. And they were all filled with the Holy Spirit and began to speak with other tongues, as the Spirit gave them utterance." (Acts 2:1-4)

Notice the words "all," "they," "them" and "each" in the passage. What they experienced here was both individual and corporate. Notice the same thing in the following passage.

"So when they heard that, they raised their voice to God with one accord and said: "Lord, You are God, who made heaven and earth and the sea, and all that is in them...And when they had prayed, the place where they were assembled together was shaken; and they were all filled with the Holy Spirit, and they spoke the word of God with boldness." (Acts 4:24,31)

When you are part of a church and stay in unity with the other members, your individual anointing is multiplied and you can accomplish more than if you were alone.

E. A Launch Pad

A local church will also provide a launch pad for your calling. As you find a place of service within the local church, God begins to train you for greater use. Your faithfulness in serving at your local church prepares you for an ever expanding circle of influence. You can be commissioned into your unique calling and also have others join to assist and support you. This was what happened to Paul and Barnabas at the beginning of their missionary ministry:

"Now in the church that was at Antioch there were certain prophets and teachers: Barnabas, Simeon who was called Niger, Lucius of Cyrene, Manaen who had been brought up with Herod the tetrarch, and Saul. As they ministered to the Lord and fasted, the Holy Spirit said, "Now separate

to Me Barnabas and Saul for the work to which I have called them." Then, having fasted and prayed, and laid hands on them, they sent them away. So, being sent out by the Holy Spirit, they went down to Seleucia, and from there they sailed to Cyprus. And when they arrived in Salamis, they preached the word of God in the synagogues of the Jews. They also had John as their assistant. "
(Acts 13:1-5).

Through their consistency in the correct local church, Barnabas and Paul were able to receive a revelation about the next step in their calling. The scriptures further confirm this point by saying,

"Those who are planted in the house of the Lord shall flourish in the courts of our God. They shall still bear fruit in old age; They shall be fresh and flourishing"
(Psalm 92:13,14)

HOW TO CHOOSE A CHURCH

Since being part of a local church is crucial to fulfilling your purpose, it is important that you locate a church that is a good fit for you. If you are already in a church and you know that it is a conducive place for growing in faith and maximizing your calling in the ways we've described, then you can skip this section. If, however, you feel dissatisfied with you current church or you are in the process of locating a church, then read on.

No Perfect Church

First of all, you must settle this fact in your mind. There is no perfect church. You will never find a church that perfectly fits every desire or expectation you have, because every church is made up of people. That is, everything that involves humanity, regardless of divine ordination, is bound to be imperfect. Since you are not perfect, your participation alone adds an element of imperfection to the church. Now think of all the other members of the church.

Many people get disillusioned at church because of some unpleasant experience that they had in church, usually related to people. The devil replays these incidents over and over in the person's mind, often succeeding in keeping people away from church, thus robbing them of the crucial support of the church in their walk of purpose.

Determine in yourself right now that you will not allow situations involving other people to rob you of your place in destiny. Make up your mind that your choice of and commitment to a church will not be determined by people but by God's confirmation in your heart of the right place for you at this season of your life.

The Choice of A Church Should Be A Spirit-Led One

While I was in college, I was part of a big college church with many people and plenty of opportunities to serve. I was even being considered as a potential leader in the church. One day, I was invited by a friend to visit a start-up church. The day I visited, there were only four of us in attendance including the pastor.

From that service and subsequent visits to this small church, I began to sense in my heart that this was the church I was meant to attend. I left the bigger church in an orderly manner and joined this small church in obedience to the witness of God's Spirit in my heart.

Looking back, that decision was one of the most consequential decisions in my life because it was in that smaller church that I met my wife and was launched into my calling in life as a pastor and teacher.

Your choice of a church should be spirit-led. It should not be primarily based on the size or resources of the church but on God's direction and witness in your heart. Not every church is conducive for your calling. A church might work for others, but not for you.

So, for example, your parents' church might not work for you. Likewise, your children's church might not be a fit for you. Along the same lines, though your friend might be thriving in a church, that church might not be the place that God ordained for you in this season.

It is important to be sensitive to the Spirit of God when making this decision. You don't just choose a church because it is close to your house or because it is more convenient to worship there or because they have interesting programs or activities. You certainly do not choose a church because it has great music, potential dates or a popular pastor.

You need to choose your church because that is the place God needs you to be at that particular time in your life for the advancement of His purpose for your life.

Also, your choice of a church should not be with a selfish motive. Though being part of a church will add a lot to your life, your approach to choosing one should not be primarily based on what you can get, but what you can contribute. Join a church that you know you can add value to through your resources, service and gifts.

Every organ of the human body contributes something. No organ is in the body as a charity case. Every organ has something to contribute, as long as it is functioning, it will be nourished. This is how church membership works too.

You should not be in a church where you have nothing to add, where everything is done for you and you just walk in and out of the services like the king of the pack. A church that will feed your destiny will demand your input. Your time, talent and treasures will be involved in the equation.

Churches are not competing grocery stores through which you should sift through, searching for the one that best meets your selfish desires. I dare say that a modification of John F. Kennedy's admonition applies in this case "Ask not what your church can do for you, but ask what you can do for your church."

The Choice of Church Should Be An Intelligent One

While I have stressed the importance of being Spirit-led in your choice of a church, it is important to note that this does not preclude using your mind intelligently. Prayerfully consider the following in making your choice of church:

1. What type of church is it?

2. What is the history of the church?

3. What are the affiliations of the church?

4. What is the stated mission of the church?

5. What are the doctrinal beliefs of the church?

6. What are the service structures of the church?

7. What is the worship style?

8. What ministries and programs are offered?

9. If you have children, what does the church offer children?

Most of these questions can be answered by attending church services a few times or by simply visiting the church's website. You may also need to talk to some people to get these facts. In your search, remember that you will not find a perfect church. Also, do not try to change a church to fit your mold. If you can't change your church then change churches.

As you locate and settle down in the local church God planned for you and begin to serve there, God will begin to develop you for your calling. Your interaction with other members will mold your character. Also, your faithfulness in service will sharpen your gifts.

Finally, your continued obedience in fulfilling little assignments will open doors for more opportunities for service. Most importantly you will be part of a family, a source of support and encouragement in the challenges in fulfilling your life's mission.

CHAPTER 4

FOUNDATIONS

"Therefore everyone who hears these words of mine and puts them into practice is like a wise man who built his house on the rock. The rain came down, the streams rose, and the winds blew and beat against that house; yet it did not fall, because it had its foundation on the rock. But everyone who hears these words of mine and does not put them into practice is like a foolish man who built his house on sand. The rain came down, the streams rose, and the winds blew and beat against that house, and it fell with a great crash." (Matthew 7:24-27 NIV)

I live in Chicago, a city that prides itself in its great architecture. The city features prominent buildings in a variety of styles designed by many renowned architects noted for their originality. One of such buildings is the John Hancock Center. "Big John," as it is colloquially called, was built in 1970 and was at one time the tallest building in the world outside New York City.

With its 100 stories, it is still one of the tallest buildings in the world. The building is home to offices and restaurants, as well as about 700 condominiums and contains the highest residences in the world. The 44th floor contains the United States' highest indoor swimming pool. The story of the construction of the John Hancock Center is a great lesson on the importance of foundations.

When the building was being constructed, it was discovered that a part of it had sunk. The work had to be suspended and the site shut down. The resulting delay caused the developers to go bankrupt.

During the shutdown, an extensive investigation was conducted, during which a fault in the original foundation was discovered. A costly remake of the foundation was the only way to correct the defects. The building eventually became an icon of engineering genius and rose up to be a major case study world-wide for deep foundations. The engineers that built it then went on to tackle the Sears Tower, currently the tallest building in the United States and the fourth tallest in the world.

I used this illustration to underscore the importance of foundations. The most important part of a building is not the edifice itself but the unseen foundation it is standing on. If the foundation is faulty, the building risks condemnation or destruction. The stronger the foundation, the more stable and versatile the building erected on it.

This is what Jesus was illustrating in the text. The foundation you build will determine the survival of your building when the storms of life come. In relation to your mission in life, the following are important foundations you must establish.

THE PRAYER FOUNDATION

Prayer is one of the most important foundational elements of your mission. The role of prayer in the fulfillment of your calling in life cannot be overemphasized. Every success in the life of a believer can be traced to a prayer success and every failure to a prayer failure.

This may sound cliché but it is true. Bathing your mission in prayer from its foundation is a sign of dependence on God. God's mission cannot be accomplished with human and natural means. It requires supernatural means. Prayer grants you access to supernatural help in carrying out your life's mission.

Unlike other endeavors, once you set yourself to pursue God's mission for your life, you will encounter many oppositions requiring divine aid to overcome. You will face many situations requiring wisdom beyond your own. Prayer is the means through which you connect to God's help.

Sailing in Shallow Waters

One of the stories that encouraged me in the early part of my ministry was told by the evangelist Reinhard Bonkke about an experience he had. He saw himself in a vision steering a big ship in shallow waters, struggling, unable to make progress and at risk of getting stuck in muddy waters.

Praying about what he saw, God told him that the ship represented his mission and he was the captain. The waters represented the operations of the Holy Spirit in his ministry. The shallow waters represented the level of God's power flowing in his ministry. It was not much.

Bonkke responded by enlisting an army of intercessors who would commit to one hour of prayer daily for his mission. Soon the ministry left the shallow waters and began to reach millions of people in various nations with mighty demonstrations of signs, wonders and miracles accompanied by the winning of many souls into the kingdom of God. Prayer unleashed the potential of his mission.

Prayer will have the same effect on your calling. Persistent prayer will take your mission from the shallow waters into the deep waters of God. The level and flow of God's power in our lives is in direct proportion to the quality of time we spend in prayer. To increase the level of God's power on your life, you must make prayer a priority.

I was also inspired by Pastor Sunday Adelaja of the Embassy of God Church, Kiev, Ukraine who God is using to do amazing things in Eastern Europe and in other parts of the world. He tells the story of how in the earlier seasons of his ministry, he committed himself to setting aside one week out of every month being away from everything, including his family, ministry and other responsibilities, to spend time alone with God.

In his time alone with God, God began to share with him secrets of changing nations with His kingdom principles and power. Soon, those secret dealings of God with him became open demonstration of power in his mission leading to the transformation of nations by God's power.

When I began to follow his example in taking time out to be with God consistently, I began to see the levels of God's operations in my life and ministry increase exponentially. Whenever, I get caught up in busyness and activities and miss these times, soon I see things begin to dry up as the active presence of God begins to wane.

The Example of Jesus

Jesus also demonstrated the importance of prayer. Though He was the Son of God and although He was occupied from day to day, morning till night, ministering to crowds, healing the sick, visiting homes, training His disciples—prayer was always a priority to Jesus. On many occasions, we see Him separating Himself to be with

God in prayer. Jesus even began His ministry with forty days of fasting and prayer in a secluded desert.

Then Jesus, being filled with the Holy Spirit, returned from the Jordan and was led by the Spirit into the wilderness, being tempted for forty days by the devil. And in those days He ate nothing, and afterward, when they had ended, He was hungry...Then Jesus returned in the power of the Spirit to Galilee, and news of Him went out through all the surrounding region. And He taught in their synagogues, being glorified by all
(Luke 4:1, 2, 14, 15)

He often withdrew from the busyness and demands of ministry to spend time with God.

However, the report went around concerning Him all the more; and great multitudes came together to hear, and to be healed by Him of their infirmities. So He Himself often withdrew into the wilderness and prayed. (Luke 5:15, 16)

When He needed to make important decisions such as choosing the twelve disciples, He spent time in prayer, sometimes through the night.

Now it came to pass in those days that He went out to the
mountain to pray, and continued all night in prayer to
God. And when it was day, He called His disciples to
Himself; and from them He chose twelve whom He also
named apostles: (Luke 6:12, 13)

In times of trial and hardship such as when He was in the garden of Gethsemane, He reached out to God in prayer.

Then they came to a place which was named Gethsemane;
and He said to His disciples, "Sit here while I pray." And
He took Peter, James, and John with Him, and He began
to be troubled and deeply distressed. ... He went a little
farther, and fell on the ground, and prayed that if it were
possible, the hour might pass from Him.
(Mark 14:32, 33, 35)

If prayer was so important and critical in the life and mission of Jesus, it ought to be more so in our lives. We must lay this foundation for the present and the future of our lives' mission.

Here are a few roles that prayer will play in your efforts to fulfill your life's mission:

A. Through prayer, you communicate with God in order to obtain His viewpoint in your decisions (See the example of David in I Samuel 30:8)

B. Prayer helps you to maintain a constant intimate connection with God and His abilities which is vital if you are going to be able to do anything worthwhile in God's name (John 15:47)

C. Through prayer you receive help to overcome devil-inspired oppositions to your mission (2 Chronicles 20:1-30, Ephesians 6:10-18)

D. Prayer changes you and helps you to be better prepared for your mission. (Genesis 32:22-30)

E. Through prayer you receive answers to petitions. You will need supplies, finances, assistance for your family and other necessities in carrying out your mission. These things are granted through prayer (Mark 11:24)

F. Prayer changes impossible situations (2 Kings 20:1-11)

G. Through prayer you can secure God's intervention in the lives of others (Acts 12:1-18, Genesis 28:16-32).

H. Prayer establishes God's will in your life and on the earth (Matthew 6:9,10)

So develop the habit of praying daily. It is one of the most crucial things you will do in your mission. You don't have to start with long hours. Start separating yourself for a few minutes daily. Practice the habit of praying without ceasing by maintaining an awareness of Him throughout your day even when you are doing other things. Involve God in all your activities by asking for His help and wisdom as you go about your daily tasks.

Saturating your life with prayer will take you a long way in accomplishing your life's mission. A wise person once said, "Satan laughs at our toiling, mocks our wisdom, but trembles when he sees the weakest saint on his knees." Prayer is the God—appointed way of carrying out His mission.

THE WORD FOUNDATION

The other foundational element you must have in place is a commitment to the word of God, which is a commitment to living your life and carrying out your mission based on the directives of God in the bible and from His Spirit. Jesus said doing what God says is like building your house on a strong foundation.

When soldiers are at war they must keep their ears open for instructions from their commanders. Instructions will flow down through the chain-of-command to the soldiers on ground. These instructions guide the conduct of war, communicate strategies and tactics. Sometimes it is to advance and at other times it is to withdraw. Any soldier that refuses to follow instructions either gets killed or punished.

In your mission too, God, your Commander-in-Chief has directives to guide you. Those directives are recorded in His word, the bible. It is your duty to familiarize yourself with them. This is why reading and studying God's word is an absolute essential in fulfilling your mission. Jesus once again exemplified this. He said:

"...Most assuredly, I say to you, the Son can do nothing of Himself, but what He sees the Father do; for whatever He does, the Son also does in like manner... I can of Myself do nothing. As I hear, I judge; and My judgment is righteous, because I do not seek My own will but the will of the Father who sent Me. (John 5:19, 30)

Jesus, in His submission to God sought to see what God was saying and doing, and only after hearing from God, did Jesus act. Everyone who is part of God's army must value God's instruction. His word must have final authority in your life. It must be your meditation— always in your heart and in your mouth. You must develop the habit of hearing His instructions and carrying them out. This is the secret of success in life and ministry. Here's how God put it to Joshua:

" Only be strong and very courageous, that you may observe to do according to all the law which Moses My servant commanded you; do not turn from it to the right hand or to the left, that you may prosper wherever you go. This Book of the Law shall not depart from your mouth, but you shall meditate in it day and night, that you may observe to do according to all that is written in it. For then you will make your way prosperous, and then you will have good success. (Joshua 1:7, 8)

Joshua was facing the daunting mission of conquering the Promised Land and dividing it amongst God's people. There were fierce battles and huge challenges ahead. You would think God would send

Joshua to military school to learn strategies. He didn't. He sent Joshua to His word.

As Joshua meditated on His Word, he would receive strength and boldness and encounter divine strategies to carry out his conquering mission. It was from his meditation on God's Word that strategies like marching around the walls of Jericho came from. They don't teach that in military school. You also have access to the wisdom of God in this way. As you meditate on His Word, you will receive divine wisdom every step of the way in your mission.

We are currently in the process of purchasing a building. At the beginning of the project, I was praying and seeking God on how to approach this when I received a strategy. While reading the story in John 2, of how Jesus turned water to wine, the spirit of God pointed my attention to the six water pots and their capacities of 20 to 30 gallons of water each.

Now there were set there six waterpots of stone, according
to the manner of purification of the Jews, containing
twenty or thirty gallons apiece. Jesus said to them, "Fill
the waterpots with water." And they filled them up to the
brim. And He said to them, "Draw some out now, and
take it to the master of the feast." And they took it.
(John 2:6-8)

My mathematical mind calculated the total capacity of all the six pots to between 120-180 pounds. My question was, why six water pots and not one? I also saw that the water pots were nearby. Incidentally the amount we needed was about $180,000.

From the passage, I got a strategy that involved us doing six categories of things to produce the money, sort of like filling six empty water pots with water which Jesus turned to wine as they drew out of them. When I implemented these things and the money began to flow in. I received the inspiration integral to my mission's success simply by meditating on the Word.

Give the Word of God priority in your mission, be it business or church work. There are principles in God's word that govern every sphere. You must locate them, exalt them and practice them. It is your source of wisdom and sustenance, your recipe for wisdom. It will ensure your success.

Blessed is the man Who walks not in the counsel of the ungodly, Nor stands in the path of sinners, Nor sits in the seat of the scornful; But his delight is in the law of the Lord, And in His law he meditates day and night. He shall be like a tree Planted by the rivers of water, That brings forth its fruit in its season, Whose leaf also shall not wither; And whatever he does shall prosper. (Psalm 1:1-3)

THE ACCOUNTABILITY FOUNDATION

The next block in your foundation is accountability. This has to do with having people in your life to whom you are answerable. Your mission will involve the handling of power. Any form of power that is unregulated is dangerous. It is a wise saying that "power corrupts and absolute power corrupts absolutely." So one of the safety valves you must establish right from the beginning of your mission is locating relationships that can inspire you and hold you accountable.

There are levels of accountability relationships. Peers can come together to be accountability partners. They practice authenticity and vulnerability regularly, praying for, supporting and correcting one another as the need arises.

Then, there is another form in which you are held accountable by someone who is an elder, precursor or forerunner in your field. Every Timothy should have a Paul, every Joshua needs a Moses, every Moses, a Jethro, every Esther, a Mordecai and every Ruth needs a Naomi. Even Jesus had John the Baptist.

Having mentors and examples that have gone ahead of you in your life is an essential for success. These people will provide safety for your mission through their counsel, prayers, and watchful accountability.

Without counsel purposes are disappointed: but in the multitude of counsellors they are established.

(Proverbs 15:22 KJV)

That ye be not slothful, but followers of them who through faith and patience inherit the promises.

(Hebrews 6:12 KJV)

As you ask God, He will arrange relationships of accountability around you. It is then your responsibility to seek these relationships and make yourself answerable to them. Never be at a point in your calling where you call all the shots. Authority is not permitted to end with you. Anyone who wields authority must also be subject to a higher authority. That is, to wield authority, you must be under authority.

THE CONSECRATION FOUNDATION

To consecrate means to make holy or to set apart. It is to designate a thing for a particular use, for which other uses apart from the designated use are unacceptable. For example, there are some of my clothes that are for special occasions only. Debo, my wife, has a set of silverware that is only brought out for use on special occasions such as Thanksgiving and Christmas. These things are consecrated!

The opposite of consecration is desecration. To desecrate is to take something separated for a particular use and use it for another purpose. It is divesting something that is sacred to a profane use.

What does this have to do with your mission? We have already seen that God separated your life for His use. To consecrate yourself means to ensure that you are living only for that purpose. It is a daily decision to lay your life on God's altar as a living sacrifice that is holy and acceptable to God (Romans 12:1).

Practically, it means you are living for only one thing, to bring glory to God and to fulfill His plans for your life. It means you are constantly depending on Him to separate yourself from sin and temptations to be motivated by any other thing apart from Him.

From the outset of your calling, you should make some quality decisions. Every sphere of a mission has its peculiar temptations. These are categorized as the lust of the eye, the lust of the flesh and the pride of life in John 2:20. They include temptations of money, sex, fame and power. These things tempt you to make your mission's focus something other than God's original intention.

Jesus faced these temptations in His ministry too. Satan came at the beginning and tempted Him, but, because He was consecrated, He was able to turn Satan down. Samson was distracted and fell under temptation. He lost everything because he failed to remain consecrated.

The Man God Uses

One of the books that has made the most impact on my life is *The Man God Uses* by Oswald J. Smith. I read it in 1992 about two years after I received my call to ministry from God. The previous two years had been a struggle for me. I knew I had an undeniable experience confirming God's call but I was reluctant to surrender to the call. I had other ambitions that I was passionate about. I was clinging to my own ideas of what my life should be about. I fell in love with science as a teenager and I was determined to pursue science with the aim of inventing something that would change the world. However, God had a different plan for my life. He had separated me for a different purpose.

So I struggled until the day that I read O. J Smith's book. I began reading it early in the morning and couldn't put it down until I finished it late at night. By the time I was done, I was on my knees weeping and dedicating myself to God and His mission only for my life. The book brought a revelation of the concept of consecration to me. It had become clear to me that the only reason why I existed was for God's use alone.

O. J Smith told the story of a particular season of his life when he was persistently praying to God to be used of him. This desire led him to study the Word of

God on the prerequisites for being mightily used of God. Although he was addressing the evangelistic ministry primarily, these qualifications apply to all assignments from God. He enumerated eleven prerequisites, three of which are related to consecration.

1. A life given over to one great purpose

2. A life from which every hindrance has been removed

3. A life placed absolutely at God's disposal

He wrote:

> Any man with divided interests, any man with many schemes, plans and programmes, any man who is interested in other things, is not going to be successful as an evangelist. The one who is going to succeed is the one who has but one great purpose in his life.
>
> Sin is bound to retard your progress. It grieves the Holy Spirit and you will never know the power of God on your life and your ministry until you are ready to renounce sin forever, to turn from it utterly and never to

indulge in it again. You will have to face that "Achan" in the camp, that idol in your heart, that habit in your life, whatever it may be. There must be a clean break. As long as you go on doing what you are now doing, God will withhold His power. His anointing you will never know and his blessing you cannot experience.

It may be that with all your talents and your gifts, all your accomplishments, all your education, you will be a complete and miserable failure in your evangelistic work, simply because there is something in your life, something in your heart, that grieves the Spirit of God and makes it impossible for Jesus Christ to use you, as He wants to, for His honor and His glory.

Let Him search you then. Let Him try you. Let Him reveal the Achan in your heart. Then confess it, put it away, and come glean with God, that He may bless and own your ministry.

All plans and ambitions; all my dreams and aspirations— all must be laid on God's altar. He must guide, direct and control my life, His will must become my will, His program mine. My future must be in His hands where

He wants me to go I must go ; I must have no plans of my own.

Are you ready to yield, to dedicate, to consecrate everything? Oh, that you would take this initial step! Be definite. Make a whole hearted surrender of your life to God. Hold nothing back. Yield up your will and accept His. There can be no substitute for your act of surrender. It is a question of signing a blank agreement.

Put your name down at the bottom and let God write the terms and conditions of the agreement after. He will only put down one step at a time and when you take that, the next step will be made plain.

It means that you sail under sealed orders. Where, you do not know. When, you cannot say. Why, is not your business. How, must not concern you. It is yours to accept from Him the sealed orders containing His blueprint for your life, and to open and read them just as He wills.

It is saying an eternal "Yes" to God and an eternal "No" to self. And it must be final that it holds good all the rest of your life. "Lord, what wilt thou have me to do? Where will thou have me to go? He dictates and you obey. One great, final, eternal, glorious Yes, and the question is forever settled. Then just keep saying " Yes" along the way. [4]

These are powerful injunctions that everyone with a desire to be used of God must heed. They certainly changed my life. From that day, I made a pact with God, yielding over my past, present and unknown future. I have been sailing under sealed orders since then.

Examples of Consecration

It is important that you lay this foundation. Decide on what you stand for before the temptations begin to roll in. Make up your mind on your boundaries.

For example, a minister tells the story of the first things that he did in his ministry being making some quality decisions that included not preaching based on financial arrangements, not borrowing money for ministry, not asking anyone for a place to preach and never compromising in the preaching of the word of God.

Mina, a Christian entertainer I know made the following commitment as her consecration to God.

> I hope to bring glory to God by always depending on the anointing of God to work and flow through me whenever I perform. I also plan to operate with a spirit of excellence in every setting that I find myself in. My prayer is that the quality of the work I do will surpass that of those who are not Ambassadors for Christ.
>
> I hope to extend the Kingdom God by being a performer with substance and purpose. The world is so used to seeing people who rely on profanity and vulgarity to entertain. However, I plan to be set apart by taking a stand. I plan to be the type of performer that can provide entertainment for an entire family. I refuse to use sexuality to sell myself or any products that I may endorse.
>
> In this information age, the ability to know facts about a celebrity's personal life are just a few clicks away. I have decided that my life outside of the stage/television will be

one that will bring glory to God. That means living a pure single life, entering into marriage with a God-fearing man, then having children - in that order. Living a lifestyle free of scandal while in the public eye will indeed extend the Kingdom.

I hope to meet the needs of people by using my ability to make people laugh. I pray that it will act as healing to those who are sick, depressed, and/or brokenhearted. My confession is that I always deliver a captivating, thought-provoking, life-changing, and hilarious performance.

In addition, I pray that my gifts take me to different places in the world and allow me to interact with different people thus, allowing me to have a certain level of influence. Nowadays, celebrities tend to have more influence in the lives of the youth than parents or traditional mentors.

While I am not satisfied with this, the facts are undeniable. I hope that having a standard will be appealing to people and that my influence will allow me to bring light to issues that concern God.

What an inspiring decision of quality! Make your own decisions. Spell out your dedication to God. Lay the foundation of consecration.

The foundation of prayer, the word of God, accountability and consecration will ensure the viability and durability of your mission. Lay it now.

CHAPTER 5

STEPPING OUT

Most assuredly, I say to you, unless a grain of wheat falls into the ground and dies, it remains alone; but if it dies, it produces much grain. (John 12:24)

After a foundation is laid, the building must then be constructed. So, the next step in the fulfillment of your assignment is to step out and start carrying it out. Start acting on your vision. Vision without action is an illusion. It is action that turns your received assignment into a real mission.

One of the traps of life is getting bogged down praying, organizing, analyzing and planning when what the time requires is action.

And the Lord said to Moses, "Why do you cry to Me? Tell the children of Israel to go forward. But lift up your rod, and stretch out your hand over the sea and divide it.

And the children of Israel shall go on dry ground through the midst of the sea. (Exodus 14:15, 16)

Praying and planning are essential, but until you take a step and start carrying out your plans, your vision will remain a daydream.

The last six letters of the word "satisfaction" spells "action." "*Satis*" is the Latin word for "enough." So satisfaction is a byproduct of enough actions. If you want to be satisfied in life and fulfill your purpose, you will need to get on your feet and start moving.

No matter how grand your vision is or how detailed your plans are, they amount to nothing if you take no steps to work them out. Without actions, you remain just a daydreamer and a dream devoid of doings is the daddy of disillusionment.

The following are a few of the forces you will have to contend with in order to jumpstart your mission.

1. THE COMFORT ZONE

Trainers train baby elephants to confine themselves to a small space by tying a rope around their legs to a pole. At first, the elephant tries to move by pulling on the rope over and over. After it has done this for a while, it resigns and accepts the fact that it cannot be free.

This resignation to its confinement continues even after it grows bigger and is able to snap the rope easily. Its repeated failure while it was a baby elephant conditions it, as an adult, to stay within a zone of comfort and limitation.

Cages of Comfort

A comfort zone is simply a self-imposed cage in which you live. The material the cage is made of is some of your many dos, don'ts, can'ts, won'ts, musts or mustn'ts. The cage is your area of familiarity and safety. Once you begin to approach the edge of this space, you become very uncomfortable and fearful. Your cage can be your pet doctrines, your limiting cherished beliefs, your family's expectations, your friends' definition of your coolness.

Or, it can be a comfortable salary as opposed to your heart's dreams, or a stable job you drag yourself to while ignoring a higher call. Similarly, it is the unhealthy relationship that you cling to because you are afraid you will be left without another option if you let go. Your comfort zone is your enemy.

God was getting ready to bless Abraham. He was going to use Him to form a nation that will bring the savior who will bless all nations. But before that could happen, Abraham would have to leave his comfort zone and begin a journey into the unknown.

A quick study will show you that Abraham was already seventy-five years old when God gave him this instruction. He was a settled man. He had seen life and lived it. He had taken roots. Using urban speak, He was in his hood, among his homeboys and peeps! But, God paid no attention to his comfortable arena. He instructed Abraham to leave. Something great was in store for Abraham out there and God was beckoning him to come get it.

What is it that you sense God telling you to do now that is outside your zone of comfort? To move to a new neighborhood or nation? To start a business or commence a ministry? To pursue your childhood dreams? To go to that school? Whatever it is, always remember that your comfort zone is a cage. It is a wall you must break through.

It is not going to be easy, but it will be worth it. It will require faith, but there is a reward. It will ruffle your feathers and disrupt your comfort, but it will bring you fulfillment. Never forget that when God wants to bless you in a new way, He doesn't drop the blessing where you currently are, rather, He deposits His blessings at a place outside your comfort zone and then beckons you to come and get them.

Step out. The fulfillment of your mission in life is outside your present cage!

2. UNCERTAINTIES

You must act even if the whole path is yet unclear. You will never see the whole path when it comes to walking with God. God operates in faith, so to walk with Him and please Him, you will also have to operate by faith (Hebrews 11:6).

Uncertainty Principle

Science, precisely quantum physics, has something called the uncertainty principle. I like to say that following God's plans for your life involves a principle of uncertainty too. There will always be a level of uncertainty regarding some aspects of your call.

God will reveal some elements of it to you but he will withhold some parts from you in order to keep your call a faith exercise. Faith pleases him. This is the reason why He will never reveal to you every aspect of His plan for your life in one sitting. Rather, He reveals it progressively as you are faithful in carrying out what He has shown you. This was the case in Abraham's call:

Now the Lord had said to Abram: "Get out of your country, From your family And from your father's house, To a land that I will show you. (Genesis 12:1)

The writer of Hebrews relates Abram's call in this way:

By faith Abraham obeyed when he was called to go out to the place which he would receive as an inheritance. And he went out, not knowing where he was going. By faith he dwelt in the land of promise as in a foreign country, dwelling in tents with Isaac and Jacob, the heirs with him of the same promise; for he waited for the city which has foundations, whose builder and maker is God. (Hebrews 11:8-10)

He went out uncertain of where he was going. He had to fight this force of uncertainty in order to begin the journey to his destiny. Everyone called of God will have to overcome this force too. You will have to step out, walking on water, so to speak, relying only on the word you have received from God. You cannot wait for everything to properly align. Things will align as you start acting. Remember,

He who observes the wind will not sow, And he who regards the clouds will not reap. (Ecclesiastes 11:4)

When you start moving, you set various things in motion. People start paying attention. Help starts to come. You begin to learn on the job. Things start getting clearer and easier. Start now, break your goals into daily little steps.

Don't just talk about it. Do it. Dust off your plans and get moving. Enroll in that course. Start that business. Take that examination. Commence that mission. Call that person. Start saving. Write that book. There will never be a better time than now.

3. INERTIA

"So Abram went, as the Lord had told him; and Lot went with him. Abram was seventy-five years old when he set out from Harran." (Genesis 12:4)

Abraham departed. He didn't equivocate, vacillate or rationalize. He got his 75- year- old body into action mode, said his goodbyes, and began his journey into the unknown land. This was faith demonstrated.

"By faith Abraham, when called to go to a place he would later receive as his inheritance, obeyed and went, even though he did not know where he was going. By faith he made his home in the promised land like a stranger in a foreign country; he lived in tents...For he was looking forward to the city with foundations, whose architect and builder is God." (Hebrews 11:8-10).

His hope of a better life, a place of promise, motivated him to step out and begin his journey even though everything was still unclear to him. God was pleased by his faith and honored it, even though he faltered later in some of his steps.

One of the biggest obstacles you will face in carrying out God's plan for your life is inertia. This is the force that wants to keep you stationed at one spot in life. It is a force that resists starting or moving, or stopping when you need to change directions. It is the enforcer of the status quo, the force of containment. It acts to reinforce the fences of your comfort zone. It is no human but it has a voice.

Whenever you hear the following words, recognize that it is Evil Inertia speaking, "you will fail", "wait for a better time", "you are too old", " you are too young", "but, nobody has ever done it before that way", "you are not qualified", "but, you don't have the capital", " but you don't have the permission", or "wait for inspiration".

You will have to break through this force and start moving. Take the first step even if it is baby-like. Begin to bite, even if it is in nibbles. Save anyhow, even if you have to start with pennies. Start from where you are. Everything starts small, from the bottom up. (The only thing that starts from the top is a hole and you are not digging a hole.) Move, even when you don't see the full path. Don't try to see the whole staircase before you start to move, just take the first step.

Steps for Starting

The following is a suggested process to go through in giving birth to a new initiative God has impressed on your heart.

1) Be submitted under the covering of a church and engage the support of your church as we discussed in Chapter 3.

2) Discover your area of passion, burden and sphere of operation from God as discussed in Chapter 2.

3) Be thoroughly informed about this area of call. Spy out the land like Moses did. Make sure you get as much facts as you can. Inquire from God. Use your mind. Research. Make sure the following questions have been resolved.

    a. Nature (What am I sent to do?)

    b. Place (Where am I to begin?)

    c. People (Who am I sent to? What are their

       needs? Who is sent with me?)

    d. Timing (When am I to start?)

    e. Approach (How do I carry it out?)

4) Set concrete goals and write them down. We are designed to be motivated by goals.

5) Create a corporate identity. Have a name for your initiative. Register the initiative with the appropriate authorities if you need to. You may also create business cards, letterhead, a website, a social networking page etc.

6) Learn from others. Shadow someone who is doing what you want to do. Attend trainings relevant to your assignment. Get educated in the line of your call.

7) Find at least one team member. Don't be a one man army. Jesus sent his disciples out in twos. Pray for the helpers you need and invest in them.

8) Initiate a meeting with people in your social jurisdiction. Starts reaching out to the people you've been sent to. Don't be afraid of starting small. Everything starts from the bottom.

9) Develop regularity in your ministry – daily, weekly, or monthly. Consistency is the key.

10) Expand your team. Find more partners who can join you.

11) Set up a support system. God will fund every assignment He gives but you must be organized. We will focus on this further in the chapter on funding your mission.

12) Reproduce it. The law of reproduction is the law of nature. God said: *"Be fruitful, multiply, and replenish the earth."*

Faith without works is dead. Actions bring the corpse of just believing to life. Jesus, in performing His miracles, always commanded some action. He told the paralyzed "take up your bed and walk." He obeyed and was healed. I picture him wriggling a little toe first, squinting his eyes, clenching his fingers, bending his knees and then jumping off the bed. He told the lepers to go and show themselves to the priest, *"and as they were going, they were cleansed"* (Luke 17:14). The key thing to note about these miracles is that they occurred as the people were moving. You must start moving too.

CHAPTER 6

RULES OF ENGAGEMENT

And also if anyone competes in athletics, he is not
crowned unless he competes according to the rules.
(2 Timothy 2:5)

I n military operations, certain rules exist to regulate the execution of missions. These are called rules of engagement. They are a set of standing orders, directives and repeatable standards on how military missions must be carried out. These rules must be obeyed by every member of the force. Violating them jeopardizes the mission and has dire repercussions.

Similarly in the execution of God's assignment for your life, there are certain laws that you must obey in order to be successful. These laws govern the execution of every mission from God regardless of the field. Both the preacher and missionary businessman must adhere to them. The scientist and educator on a mission from God must obey them. They are universal laws that everyone in God's missionary force must observe. They guarantee success in your assignment.

These laws are not man's laws but principles and rules derived from scriptural injunctions. Since every verse of scripture is inspired by God, carrying His authority, those passages of scripture that address the nature and execution of ministry are necessarily divine laws that we must honor and observe.

HOW I CAME BY THESE LAWS

A particular time in our ministry, I faced many challenges that came from various directions. It seemed many things I had been taught and was applying in ministry were not working. I became disillusioned and many times was tempted to quit. My frustration drove me to an extended time of prayer and concentrated study of the word of God and other anointed materials. My quest during this season of seeking God was to find out His prescriptions for success in ministry.

As I read accounts of people who were sent of God in scriptures, biographies of great men of God and other books addressing exploits in ministry, I began to see certain patterns. I saw that the principles espoused by the lives and ministries of these greats could be categorized and condensed into a set of laws that every one called of God could follow in order to be successful in their individual callings.

These laws are universal. God is no respecter of persons but He is a respecter of His principles. Those who align themselves with His ways will enjoy His favor and backing without favoritism.

Then Peter opened his mouth and said: "In truth I perceive that God shows no partiality. But in every nation whoever fears Him and works righteousness is accepted by Him. (Acts 10:34, 35)

In other words, scriptural principles have as much potency in America as in Africa, Asia or parts of the world. They are not affected or distorted by variations in weather, culture or infrastructure. The methods of applying them may differ, but the principles work consistently independent of lands and climes.

Isn't it reassuring to know that you are not limited because of your background or natural origin, that some people are not more privileged than you? You have as much right to succeed in your calling as any other child of God because God is rich unto all that call on Him.

For the Scripture says, "Whoever believes on Him will not be put to shame." For there is no distinction between Jew and Greek, for the same Lord over all is rich to all who call upon Him. For "whoever calls on the name of the Lord shall be saved." (Romans 10:11-13)

He is the same Lord over all and He is favorably disposed toward everyone who calls on Him in truth. He answers without discrimination based on the caller's

116

earthly circumstances. Thus, ministry can be successful in any nation. There are no dry lands where the principles of God go to waste. Yes, in some lands, it might take more time, require more effort in cultivation, call for unique methods, but God's ways will always triumph everywhere. Outcomes will vary, methods will be diverse, but success is guaranteed to everyone who follows God's way.

Yes, some of these laws of God are easier to apply in some settings than others. I have been privileged of God to live and pastor both in Africa and North America. I have seen that in Africa, because of the infrastructural deficiencies and the still evolving order in society, the principle of God-dependence is almost mandatory if one is to survive.

On the other hand, in America, people have many false alternatives like governmental assistance and the credit system. These sometimes compete with an absolute focus on God.

However, I have seen from experience that when applied, the principles of ministry hold true in both continents. Let's examine these laws.

1. THE LAW OF THE OVERFLOW

This law simply states that success in ministry with men is an overflow of your success in union with God. I have studied successful men in ministry, both in the Bible and in history. I observed that all those who had great and lasting impact on humanity for God had a depth of relationship with God beyond the ordinary.

Abraham was called the friend of God. Jacob had to prevail with God before he could prevail with men. God spoke to Moses face-to-face as a man speaks to a friend. Joshua received divine strategies as he communed with God. David was a man after God's heart. Paul's one pursuit was to know Him and the power of His resurrection. John was a lover of His presence.

I have this as one of my ministry philosophies. I tell myself, "The ultimate goal of my life is to know Him

118

and love Him. If I love Him with all my heart, soul and mind, there is no place for any other love except the love He chooses to show through me. This is my only ministry. Every other ministry is the one He chooses to do through me, an overflow of this primary ministry. I will focus on loving Him and He will love people through me. I will never exalt my service to people above my relationship with Him. He must be pre-eminent. "This is the one needful thing" (Luke 10:41).

Great historical figures used mightily of God like William Tyndale, John Huss, Francis of Assisi, Martin Luther, Count Zinzendorf, John Wesley, William Wilberforce, Charles Finney, D.L Moody to mention a few were all men who pursued and developed rare depths of relationship with God.

Their effective ministries to men were overflows of their deep personal encounters with God. Because God knew them and they knew Him, He could trust them with much.

D.L Moody said, *"Make Christ first. Make Christ the cornerstone of your life. Live in Christ and the light on this hill will shine around the world."*

If you want a lasting ministry of impact then you must not ignore this rule. You cannot give what you don't have. Peter said to the lame man at the beautiful gate,

> *Then Peter said, "Silver and gold I do not have, but what I do have I give you: In the name of Jesus Christ of Nazareth, rise up and walk." (Acts 3:6)*

Until God has reached you, you can't reach anyone. You must be edified in order to edify others. Until He has touched you, you can't touch anyone. The things you have not seen, touched, nor handled, you cannot impart to others. John said,

> *That which was from the beginning, which we have heard, which we have seen with our eyes, which we have looked upon, and our hands have handled, concerning the Word of life... that which we have seen and heard we declare to you, that you also may have fellowship with us; and truly*

our fellowship is with the Father and with His Son Jesus Christ. (1 John 1:1, 3).

God calls us to Himself first before He sends us to others.

And He called the twelve to Himself, and began to send them out two by two, and gave them power over unclean spirits. (Mark 6:7)

Ministry is digging into the heart of God, to reach out to men. It is the overflow of the God-influence on you to others. It is the glory of God shinning from your face to others because you have been communing with the Lord of glory and He has radiated you first with His glory.

So he was there with the Lord forty days and forty nights; he neither ate bread nor drank water. And He wrote on the tablets the words of the covenant, the Ten Commandments. Now it was so, when Moses came down from Mount Sinai (and the two tablets of the Testimony were in Moses' hand when he came down from the mountain), that Moses did not know that the skin of his face shone while he talked with Him. So when Aaron and all the children of Israel saw Moses, behold, the skin of his face shone, and they were afraid to come near him.

(Exodus 34:28-30)

The early apostles knew this law. When they were faced with the choice of serving food to the people and focusing on being with God, they said,

"It is not desirable that we should leave the word of God and serve tables. Therefore, brethren, seek out from among you seven men of good reputation, full of the Holy Spirit and wisdom, whom we may appoint over this business; but we will give ourselves continually to prayer and to the ministry of the word." (Acts 6:2-4).

No wonder people noticed the difference in Peter and John.

Now when they saw the boldness of Peter and John, and perceived that they were uneducated and untrained men, they marveled. And they realized that they had been with Jesus. And seeing the man who had been healed standing

with them, they could say nothing against it.

(Acts 4:13, 14)

People traced Peter and John's miraculous ministries back to these disciples' association with Jesus. Your ministry is a byproduct of your relationship with God—this is the first law of ministry. Obey it. Get in His presence.

Commit to pursuing quality fellowship with Him, investing time in prayer and searching His word. His impact on your life will overflow to nations and generations after you.

2. THE LAW OF ALIGNMENT

The law of alignment says there is a pattern of God for every divine assignment; building according to this pattern will ensure the maximum backing of God. This law has to do with the accuracy of your pursuit, its alignment with the plans, purposes and motivations of God. The more aligned you are with Him in your pursuit, the more of His blessing you will see in your ministry.

In his book, Plans, Purposes and Pursuits, Kenneth Hagin wrote of a visitation he received from the Lord Jesus. The revelation from the vision was about how people devise their own plans and then ask God to bless them, rather than seek His plans and purposes for them and their ministries. Because the plans are not God's, He cannot bless them.

This is because the pursuit is not fully aligned with His will. God said if people would seek His plans and pursue them with His purpose, He would bless their pursuits and things will work almost like clockwork.

And see to it that you make them according to the pattern which was shown you on the mountain. (Exodus 25:40)

God's pattern for your assignment is unique. You can be inspired by others and motivated by what they are doing or have done, however, you cannot just copy everything you see others doing. You must filter all your role models through the funnel of God's pattern for your mission. Because your best friend is on Television does not mean you have to be on TV. God's army is ordered with everyone having their places and unique assignments.

They run like mighty men, They climb the wall like men of war; Every one marches in formation, And they do not break ranks. (Joel 2:7).

Find your place and stay there. Crossing lanes in the race leads to disqualification. Intrusion in an assignment that is not yours is deadly. Just ask Uzzah who broke the due order of God, trying to save the ark, intruding in an assignment that wasn't his.

And when they came to Nachon's threshing floor, Uzzah put out his hand to the ark of God and took hold of it, for the oxen stumbled. Then the anger of the Lord was aroused against Uzzah, and God struck him there for his error; and he died there by the ark of God.

(2 Samuel 6:6, 7)

The reason for Uzzah's death was later confirmed by David.

Then David said, "No one may carry the ark of God but the Levites, for the Lord has chosen them to carry the ark of God and to minister before Him forever." He said to them, "You are the heads of the fathers' houses of the Levites; sanctify yourselves, you and your brethren, that you may bring up the ark of the Lord God of Israel to the place I have prepared for it. For because you did not do it the first time, the Lord our God broke out against us, because we did not consult Him about the proper order."
(1 Chronicles 15:2, 12, 13).

God has a proper order. Stop doing things as convenient. Do them as commanded (1 Samuel 13:11-14). Consult with Him on it. When you receive His plan, pursue it with His purpose and motivation and you will see His blessings in your ministry.

3. THE LAW OF ABSOLUTE DEPENDENCE

This law has to do with humility and trust as opposed to pride and self-sufficiency. It states that God's mission can only be successfully executed with God's ability.

So he answered and said to me: "This is the word of the Lord to Zerubbabel: 'Not by might nor by power, but by My Spirit,' Says the Lord of hosts. (Zechariah 4:6).

Jesus said, "without me you can do nothing." (John 15:5). Ministry carried out with man's wisdom, human-inspired methods or gimmicks is going nowhere. It will lack authentic fruit. It takes God to bear God-fruits.

The great evangelist T.L Osborn tells the story of his early days of ministry when he and his wife Daisy, tried all they could as missionaries to India but could not win a single soul to Christ. They returned to America, frustrated.

Shortly after then, they had an encounter with Christ that transformed them and their ministries. Years of fruitfulness followed as they began to operate in the power of the Holy Spirit.

If you are going to be successful in your assignment, you will have to let go of your self-sufficiency to fully depend on God's strength. Your education, eloquence, wit, popularity, good looks or personal charm will not take you as far as God can.

Your title or position is not enough. You need God's help, not man's. He is the one who called you and with His call comes the resources you need to carry it out. Looking elsewhere, either to yourself or others will limit you.

God graciously trains His servants in dependence. He will allow you to come to the end of yourself as all your self-efforts fail to produce real results until you cry out for His help. Then, He will step in. Until Joseph acknowledged God, not himself, as the only one capable of interpreting of dreams, he was kept locked in prison.

*And Pharaoh said to Joseph, "I have had a dream, and
there is no one who can interpret it. But I have heard it
said of you that you can understand a dream, to interpret
it." So Joseph answered Pharaoh, saying, " It is not in me;
God will give Pharaoh an answer of peace." (Genesis
41:15, 16)*

Humility is endearing to God. He resists the
proud but gives grace to the humble. He never intended
ministry to be done with human strength but by divine
enabling. Without Him, your work is like wood without
fire, withering grasses without the dew of heaven—your
words will produce no conviction. Endeavor to have a
Spirit-empowered ministry. Put your total dependence
on the Holy Spirit and learn to work in cooperation with
Him.

4. THE LAW OF THE SUPREMACY OF THE WORD

This law speaks to the exaltation of the Word of
God in every aspect of life and ministry. Everything in
your ministry must have its origin in the word of God

and be founded and built on it. The Word of God must be the final authority, the supreme arbiter in all matters.

I will bow down toward your holy temple and will praise your name for your love and your faithfulness, for you have exalted above all things your name and your word (Psalm 138:20)

It is from it that you derive your plans and strategies. It is your menu for success-your meditation and delight. You comply with its directives and exalt them above all human tradition and opinions. You study it diligently to show yourself approved. You live it and preach it uncompromisingly. If your ministry is from the Word, and remains in the Word, it is bound to be successful.

God gave Joshua the secret of success at the beginning of his ministry. It was the simple command:

This Book of the Law shall not depart from your mouth, but you shall meditate in it day and night, that you may observe to do according to all that is written in it. For then

you will make your way prosperous, and then you will
have good success. (Joshua 1:8).

Success in Joshua's ministry meant conquering lands and dividing them to God's people. It meant achieving what the whole generation before could not achieve and it was to come by his commitment to the Word of God.

Paul told Timothy almost exactly the same thing.

"Till I come, give attention to reading, to exhortation, to
doctrine. Do not neglect the gift that is in you, which was
given to you by prophecy with the laying on of the hands
of the eldership. Meditate on these things; give yourself
entirely to them, that your progress may be evident to all.
(1 Timothy 4:13-15)"

Exalting the word of God will produce evident progress in your ministry.

5. THE LAW OF FOCUS

In order to be successful in your mission, you must be a person of one pursuit. That is, you must be single-minded, focused on your life-mission. This is the law of focus. Peter told Jesus, "... "See, we have left all and followed You." (Mark 10:28). Before he met Jesus, Peter was a fisherman. Then he received Jesus' call to leave everything and follow Him.

And Jesus, walking by the Sea of Galilee, saw two brothers, Simon called Peter, and Andrew his brother, casting a net into the sea; for they were fishermen. Then He said to them, "Follow Me, and I will make you fishers of men." They immediately left their nets and followed Him. (Matthew 4:18-20)

Peter left every other thing in order to pursue his call. He made it his one focus.

In order for you to fulfill your mission on earth, you will also need to have one focus. Granted, you will have many roles to play in life, but your eyes should be fixed on your goal. Everything in your life must fit into that high call of God you have received. Your eyes must be on the trophy at the end of your life. Your focus must be to please Him who called you into His army.

No one engaged in warfare entangles himself with the affairs of this life, that he may please him who enlisted him as a soldier. (2 Timothy 2:4)

Once you've made the decision to follow God's plan for your life, refuse to look back or around. Burn the bridge to your past. Don't be bothered by people's opinions or the pace of other people in their own race. Run your race with your eyes fixed on Jesus. Cut off from every encumbrance. Make your call your focus. Abandon your whole life to the Lord.

Paul demonstrates this law by saying,

Not that I have already attained, or am already perfected; but I press on, that I may lay hold of that for which Christ Jesus has also laid hold of me. Brethren, I do not count myself to have apprehended; but one thing I do,

133

forgetting those things which are behind and reaching forward to those things which are ahead, I press toward the goal for the prize of the upward call of God in Christ Jesus. (Philippians 3:12-14)

This should be your attitude toward your call too. There are many distractions on the path of purpose, many of them legitimate. You will have plenty of opportunities to deviate, to do other things apart from what He has sent you to do. But, you will need to set your face like flint.

" For the Lord GOD will help Me; Therefore I will not be disgraced; Therefore I have set My face like a flint, And I know that I will not be ashamed. (Isaiah 50:7)

Now it came to pass, when the time had come for Him to be received up, that He steadfastly set His face to go to Jerusalem, (Luke 9:51)

Refuse to be moved off the way. If you miss it, get back immediately as soon as you realize your focus is split. Your assignment in life requires your complete focus.

6. THE LAW OF INTEGRITY

The strength and foundation of ministry is integrity. Without it everything crumbles. Integrity is the quality of being honest and having strong moral principles. It is synonymous with character. A minister without integrity is going nowhere. Without integrity there is no ascension to the highest levels of God's call. This the law of integrity.

Who may ascend into the hill of the Lord? Or who may stand in His holy place? He who has clean hands and a pure heart, Who has not lifted up his soul to an idol, Nor sworn deceitfully. (Psalm 24:3, 4).

Many mighty men and women of God have fallen because of a lack of integrity. Great enterprises have collapsed because they were compromised. Think of what sin has done to many who had great calls from the

Lord: Samson, Saul and Judas to name a few. It limits, shames and destroys.

In recent times, we saw the dissolution of Arthur Andersen, one of the five largest accounting companies in the world, in existence for almost a century, with 85,000 employees worldwide, because integrity appeared to be abandoned in their auditing processes.

Untouchables

Depart! Depart! Go out from there, Touch no unclean thing; Go out from the midst of her, Be clean, You who bear the vessels of the Lord. (Isaiah 52:11)

Bearing God's vessel is being on mission with Him. The same language was used in referring to Paul's call in the following passage,

But the Lord said to him, "Go, for he is a chosen vessel of Mine to bear My name before Gentiles, kings, and the children of Israel. (Acts 9:15).

What are these untouchables? As I once heard someone say, "we must not touch His glory, His girls or His gold!" These symbolize pride, sexual and financial improprieties. These three daggers have struck more ministers than can be counted. If we are going to be ultimately successful in our mission, we must keep our ministry pure in every way. Our integrity is seen in who we are when no one is looking. It is different from reputation. Your reputation will eventually fall or rise to the level of your integrity.

God extends His grace, developing our characters if we let Him. The fruit of the Spirit enumerated by Paul are the contents of character.

I say then: Walk in the Spirit, and you shall not fulfill the lust of the flesh. For the flesh lusts against the Spirit, and the Spirit against the flesh; and these are contrary to one another, so that you do not do the things that you wish. But the fruit of the Spirit is love, joy, peace, longsuffering, kindness, goodness, faithfulness, gentleness, self-control. Against such there is no law. (Galatians 5:16, 17, 22, 23).

Fruits grow. As we commit ourselves to God and allow His Spirit to mold us, these traits will begin to grow in our lives and find expression in our affairs. The more this happens, the greater the likelihood of success in our missions.

7. THE LAW OF SACRIFICE

Sacrifice is the forfeiture of something highly valued for the sake of one considered to have a greater value or claim. Students give up sleep, years of their life and recreation time in hope of a degree. Athletes give up certain things in order to prepare for the competition with the hope of winning a medal. That's sacrifice.

Your calling comes with sacrifice too. When Jesus called, He always made it plain to those He called that He wasn't calling them to a life of ease and self-indulgence. The rich young ruler was told to sell his goods. The family man was told to let the dead bury their dead. He tells all clearly that the call will cost them something. It would eventually pay more, but at the outset, some sacrifice will be required.

The call of God on your life will sometimes be costly, inconvenient and demanding. It will ask for something you treasure before it releases its treasures to you.

Often in obeying God's call, you will have to leave something. Abraham had to leave his country and relatives. Moses had to forsake the pleasure of being the prince of Egypt, to suffer affliction with God's people in the wilderness. Jesus left the glories of heaven and made Himself of no reputation, humbling Himself like a servant to the point of death. Peter and the other apostles left their vocations and homes. They were persecuted and hated.

Ministry that costs nothing accomplishes nothing. The measure of a ministry consists of the sacrifices made to carry it out. The Apostle Paul speaking of the worth of his ministry listed things that he had to endure.

We give no offense in anything, that our ministry may not be blamed. But in all things we commend ourselves as ministers of God: in much patience, in tribulations, in needs, in distresses, in stripes, in imprisonments, in tumults, in labors, in sleeplessness, in fastings; by the word of truth, by the power of God, by the armor of righteousness on the right hand and on the left, by honor and dishonor, by evil report and good report; as deceivers, and yet true; as sorrowful, yet always rejoicing; as poor, yet making many rich; as having nothing, and yet possessing all things. (2 Corinthians 6:3-5, 7, 8, 10)

Paul is celebrated as one of the greatest generals of God and deservedly so because the greatest generals are the ones with the most scars. His ministry was characterized by sacrifice. Paul uses the word death to describe it (1 Corinthians 15:3). There can be no life without death; no fruit without seeds. You have to give up to go up.

So brace up yourself to give everything you've got into your call. Be diligent. Work hard. Labor in God's grace. There is a reward on the other side of sacrifice. Your call may require you to give up some comfort or pleasure. It may ask for your accomplishments and degrees; your personal plans and ambitions. It may demand your finances and possessions. It will require a substantial input of your time and energy.

Give it whatever it demands. It is worth it and the price can never be greater than God's grace and the ultimate reward. Your input are seeds and according to God's law, seedtime is always followed by harvest time. After sowing comes reaping. After bearing precious seeds weeping, comes the returning with the sheafs in joy. This is the cycle of life.

Then Peter began to say to Him, "See, we have left all and followed You." So Jesus answered and said, "Assuredly, I say to you, there is no one who has left house or brothers or sisters or father or mother or wife or children or lands, for My sake and the gospel's, who shall not receive a hundredfold now in this time—houses and brothers and sisters and mothers and children and lands, with

persecutions—and in the age to come, eternal life.
(Mark 10:28-30).

8. THE LAW OF FOLLOWERSHIP

Followership is capacity or willingness to follow another person. It is the practice of allowing yourself to be led. Obviously it is not a popular concept because it implies being behind or below some other person.

Most people get excited about leadership because it puts you in front and in command, but if you want to be a great leader, you must first become a great follower. The greatest leaders are the best followers and true leadership always begins by following. Joshua was the follower of Moses, Elisha followed Elijah, the early apostles followed Jesus.

"And Jesus, walking by the Sea of Galilee, saw two brothers, Simon called Peter, and Andrew his brother, casting a net into the sea; for they were fishermen. Then He said to them, "Follow Me, and I will make you fishers

of men." They immediately left their nets and followed Him." (Matthew 4:19, 20).

Jesus, the greatest of all leaders followed his father to the point of death. He even subjected himself to follow John the Baptist as his forerunner. A life void of influences is a failure, because it doesn't influence anyone. To be a great leader you must be a great follower. You cannot wield legitimate authority when you are not under any authority yourself. Every form of power must have control or it becomes a danger to those exposed to its influence.

There is no self-made person. Every person is a product of others. If you want to be a reference in your ministry then you must have references. Everyone who aspires to be a great teacher must remain a dedicated student. If you want to be a model then you must follow some model. The legitimacy of your leadership is rooted in your followership.

The only person who is preeminent is God. He is the only one who deserves first place. He is the only one who can legitimately be called the Most High because He came before all and in Him everything consists. The rest of creation has to fall in line somewhere in the ranks.

Lucifer failed to obey this law and ended up as the scum of creation. He forgot his place and in pride chose to personally remove himself from following God. Now he has to follow even little children who wield the name of Jesus. This is a tragedy of pride.

But He gives more grace. Therefore He says: "God resists the proud, But he gives grace to the humble." (James 4:6)

Being willing to follow is a demonstration of humility, therefore it gives access to more grace. Grace is God's ability working on behalf of a person. Submitting yourself to the Law of Followership releases this ability. The way up is down. Jesus earned the right to have the most honored name because He willingly followed the Father to humiliation and death on the cross.

Let this mind be in you which was also in Christ Jesus,

but made Himself of no reputation, taking the form of a

bondservant, and coming in the likeness of men. And

being found in appearance as a man, He humbled Himself

and became obedient to the point of death, even the

death of the cross. Therefore God also has highly exalted

Him and given Him the name which is above every name,

that at the name of Jesus every knee should bow, of those

in heaven, and of those on earth, and of those under the

earth, and that every tongue should confess that Jesus

Christ is Lord, to the glory of God the Father.

(Philippians 2:5, 7-11)

If you want your ministry to have great authority
Here are some practical ways you can apply this law in
your ministry.

How to Practice Followership

1. Follow the written word of God and the dictates of the
Spirit of God. Be compliant with any standing
instructions of God to you and take the position of
willingness to obey any instruction from him that may

come in the future, no matter what obeying them will demand. Let His will be preeminent in your life.

As you read these words, the Spirit of God may be bringing some specific things to your mind that He had impressed on your heart in the past but which you never heeded. These unheeded instructions are like applied brakes in your vehicle of followership that must be disengaged for you to go to the next level in your ministry.

At a time in my ministry, I applied the brakes in the area of writing for some reasons, chief of which was that I wasn't impressed with my writing. I was waiting for the time when I would become a more impressive writer before I embarked on writing the various book ideas God kept on giving me. I knew writing was something God wanted me to do but I was unwilling to do it because I wanted things to be perfect. This led to a couple of years of feeling unfulfilled and unhappy because I was not acting on a key pillar of my mission on earth.

This continued until I was able to release the breaks in my followership in this area at training with Pastor Sunday Adelaja in Kiev, Ukraine. I have been writing since then and the rewards of following have been amazing.

2. Follow Someone.

That ye be not slothful, but followers of them who through faith and patience inherit the promises." (Hebrews 6:12).

Mentorship is a corollary of the law of followership. Everyone who will be successful must have models and mentors. The word "mentor" has its roots in Greek mythology.

In the Odyssey, Mentor was the loyal adviser of Odysseus that he entrusted with the care and education of Telemachus his son while he was on his famous and long journey. A mentor is therefore a wise and trusted counselor or teacher. A mentor is someone who trains a person with lesser experience or knowledge than him. Mentors are God's gift to your calling.

Having a mentor provides you with a model of what you could be or even exceed. It exposes you to a higher level of accomplishment and wisdom. It is protective because you have access to wise counsels that can save you from making costly mistakes. It gives your mission credibility and multiplies your productivity exponentially.

All the great people I have met and read about always point to someone ahead of them that they follow and emulate. Timothy had Paul. Esther had Mordecai. Moses would have died from exhaustion were it not for Jethro's mentorship. I thank God for the mentors God has given me. They continue to make the accomplishment of my life's mission realizable through their prayers, guidance and corrections.

3. Be an Untiring Student

You also practice following by your insatiable hunger for knowledge and wisdom. There is nothing new under the sun. Every challenge you face now or will face in the future has already been faced and documented by someone. The knowledge you need for the next level in your ministry is already in a particular book or resource somewhere.

Seek out those resources. Be an addicted student. Study the work of others. Read books voraciously. Readers are leaders and leaders are readers. Anyone that will make impact in the world must be a student of those who have gone ahead.

Jesus demonstrated this at age twelve when He was with the doctors and teachers in the temple asking them questions. It is those who ask questions that become answers. It is seekers of knowledge that are eventually sought out. Go ahead. Stock up your library and immerse yourself in the study of great works. In there, greatness will rub off on you and will find expression in your ministry.

Practice these and you will be engaging the law of followership in your ministry with great benefits following.

9. THE LAW OF FAITH

This is a very important law. It is not just a law of ministry but the law of life itself. The scriptures repeats in four different passages that, "the just shall live by faith...." (Hebrews 10:38). So faith is the way of life of the believer. Faith is our lifeline. Without faith, God is not impressed (Hebrews 11:6) and without faith there is no exploit in ministry.

Everything God will bestow on your ministry will have to be received by faith. Faith is what translates heavenly realities into earthly tangibles. Faith makes everything work. Without faith, prayers are empty words (Mark 11:23-24), access to the divine resources of grace is impossible (Romans 5:1-2), there is no victory (I John

5:4), the fiery arrows of the enemy hit their targets (Ephesians 6:16) and even salvation is impossible (Ephesians 2:8).

Faith is the currency of heaven. It is the legal tender that we exchange to the hope of our mission in life. Your destination is a promise. Faith is what delivers God's promises to you. It is obvious from scriptures that your level of results in ministry is "according to your faith."

How do you engage this law in your mission? First, you have to build faith. Faith is built by hearing the word of God (Romans 10:17). God's word is pregnant with faith so when you give it attention by hearing it enough, it will impregnate you with living faith. Secondly, faith must be released. Faith is released through corresponding actions, by doing what God's word says with confident expectation that you have what it promises. This release of faith then causes things to move from the unseen realm into the seen.

Faith is your weapon of success in ministry. It is your access to your promised destiny. Go for it. Study more about it. Build it and keep it released. God will honor your confidence in Him.

10. THE LAW OF COMPASSION

Recently, while I was studying the earthly ministry of Jesus, I noticed a repeating mention of His compassion. A couple of examples,

And when Jesus went out He saw a great multitude; and He was moved with compassion for them, and healed their sick. (Matthew 14:14)

Then Jesus, moved with compassion, stretched out His hand and touched him, and said to him, "I am willing; be cleansed." (Mark 1:41)

And Jesus, when He came out, saw a great multitude and was moved with compassion for them, because they were like sheep not having a shepherd. So He began to teach them many things. (Mark 6:34)

So Jesus had compassion and touched their eyes. And immediately their eyes received sight, and they followed Him. (Matthew 20:34)

I saw that Jesus taught, healed, fed people and raised the dead motivated by compassion. In fact, I could see compassion as the motivation of His entire mission from heaven to earth, to the cross, the grave and back to heaven.

Now He is seated in heaven as our compassionate high priest making intercession for us. The light came on in me. I understood that if the master's motivation for His mission was compassion, then since we are called to continue His mission, we cannot succeed with any other motivation.

Compassion is love in action. It is not just pity or sympathy. It is active empathy. It is not just a thing but the very essence of God Himself who is love and full of compassion. Compassion is God touching people through you. It is the law that unleashes the anointing.

When true compassion is in play, the power of God surges on the scene.

I remember a time when I was praying for one of the members of a church I was pastoring who was experiencing a serious health crisis and was nearing the point of death.

When I saw his state, something came over me and I locked myself up in my room and began to cry out to God for healing. God graciously answered and he was healed. He is still going on strong and in the ministry right now planting churches. Glory to God! Compassion will open up your ministry to the miraculous because you will be tapping into the very heart of God for His creation.

How do you develop compassion? First, spend sufficient time with Compassion Himself, God, and He will start rubbing off on you. You will begin to develop His heart for people. Second, expose yourself to the

154

needs of the people you are sent to. Compassion stirs in you when you make contact with needs.

We cannot succeed in ministry if our goal is to use people to achieve our ends. Selfishness will not bear God's stamp of approval. Any ministry that is motivated by any other thing but love is unacceptable before God. The motive for ministry cannot be fame, financial gains or any other selfish reason. These will not be blessed by God.

For even the Son of Man did not come to be served, but to serve and to give His life a ransom for many."
(Mark 10:45)

That is our perfect model for ministry. These laws are certainly not the only laws that govern our mission but they are definitely some of the most consequential. Apply them in your ministry and let obedience propel you into new levels of effectiveness in your assignment.

CHAPTER 7

FUNDING YOUR MISSION

And He said to them, "When I sent you without money
bag, knapsack, and sandals, did you lack anything?" So
they said, "Nothing." (Luke 22:35)

M any individuals thinking of stepping out and doing something they believe God has called them to do have certain areas of uncertainty that they battle with, the biggest of them all being the issue of funding.

It is safe to say that many people are stuck in jobs they don't like or are practically stopped on their tracks because of the fear of starting and not having the resources they need to sustain themselves and their ministries.

I have faced the same fears several times in my life. The first time it was significantly pronounced when I was to begin pastoring a recent church plant in Lagos, Nigeria then. I could not work professionally because I was still an undergraduate engineering student at the time combining ministry work with school.

Pastoring the church meant that I was going to be the person in charge of overseeing the financial responsibilities of the church which included the maintenance of its building and some part-time and a couple of full-time staff including myself. The church had just started two years prior so it didn't have much in terms of savings or investments.

Here I was, a young pastor, learning to trust God for resources to keep the expanding ministries of the church moving. I remember having to trust God weekly to pay the staff, my living expenses and still have budget allocations for the ministry projects of the church. It was at this time that God intensified the lessons He had been teaching me about ministry finances while I pastored a college fellowship for some years before this church. I came across some basic principles in the word of God on funding any mission that God has sent you to do.

I pastored this church for about three years and during those years I saw how God was faithful in providing abundantly for all the needs of the ministry. My next assignment was in the United States. I moved to Chicago (at God's leading, to join my wife who just finished her college studies) unsure of exactly what I was going to do, but knowing that God had some assignment for us to do here.

When I arrived in Chicago, I had just $150 on me and two boxes full of books. I immediately began to teach at a weekly gathering of some young people who were part of my wife's college and work network. Some months after this, I was part of another church plant where I served as associate pastor until God summoned me to start the CityLight Church.

During the time of preparation to start the CityLight Church, that sense of uncertainty reared its head again. This time it was more pronounced because I was already adjusted to the comfort zone of receiving some kind of steady salary from my ministerial work as an associate pastor and we now had Jesse, our first son, and my wife was pregnant with Joshua, our second, at the time.

We were going to have to step out and start the church with no visible channel of support. Through God's grace we did. God began to show his faithfulness to this assignment from the beginning.

Shortly after we decided to obey God, one of the people I had pastored before called me and gave me a check of $1,000 for the church. That was the first gift to the church. We used that to pay for a meeting venue, purchase some equipment and then we ran out of money. All the people on our team apart from Debo were students or unemployed at the time so there was no talk of receiving any substantial offering.

A day before we had our first public service, I was almost getting discouraged because we had run out of money and there were things to be done requiring more funds.

I had also invited my mentor, Pastor Sam Adeyemi to commission the church. He had traveled all the way from Nigeria to be at the event and had just arrived at his hotel room. I went into the room to welcome him. When I was about to leave, he handed me an envelope saying it was from his church to our new church. I thanked him.

When I got out, I opened the envelope and found that it was a gift of $3,000 from Daystar Church in Lagos to the yet-to-start CityLight Church. I immediately told my wife and other team members. That amount was more than enough for us to handle the starting expenses of the church. However, it did more than supply a need, it eliminated in me forever the fear of not having supplies for ministry and since then God has used that gift to remind me of His backing of the mission whenever we wanted to do something new that required a stretch in our financial capacity.

Over the years as I have pastored the church, we've seen God supply our needs in amazing and sometimes unusual ways. We have had individuals we do not know send in money and resources. We've had several corporate entities, send in tens of thousands of dollars in cash and non-cash resources to fund our compassionate outreaches to the economically depressed residents of the city.

At one time when we were setting up a new office facility, a company sent in several ready cubicles worth several thousands of dollars for us to install for free. We have had churches send in thousands of dollars in cash and other wish list resources. Other non-profit organizations like Campus Crusade, Moody Bible

Institute, to mention a few regularly partner with us in outreaches supplying both human and material resources. There is still more to be done and more resources needed for prospective phases of the mission, but from our experience, I can say that we've proven that when God sends you on a mission, He provides.

Now I'm telling you this story because in this chapter, I want to share with you some of the truths I have learned about funding your mission. First, let's examine some basic concepts.

INSTANCES OF MISSION FUNDING IN GOD'S WORD

Just to inspire your faith, I want to lay out some of the key instances in the bible when people were sent by God on some sort of assignment and how God supplied the needs for the assignment. I want to make a case that God always funds missions that He commissions.

1. The First Assignment Plus a Wife

The first assignment of God to any human was to Adam in the book of Genesis. His assignment was to govern the earth and to tend and guard the garden of Eden. We see that God had all the resources he needed to carry this out prepared even before Adam showed up on the scene.

The Lord God planted a garden eastward in Eden, and there He put the man whom He had formed. And out of the ground the Lord God made every tree grow that is pleasant to the sight and good for food. The tree of life was also in the midst of the garden, and the tree of the knowledge of good and evil. Then the Lord God took the man and put him in the garden of Eden to tend and keep it. And the Lord God commanded the man, saying, "Of every tree of the garden you may freely eat; but of the tree of the knowledge of good and evil you shall not eat, for in the day that you eat of it you shall surely die." And the Lord God said, " It is not good that man should be alone;

I will make him a helper comparable to him."
(Genesis 2:8, 9, 15-18).

And God said, "See, I have given you every herb that
yields seed which is on the face of all the earth, and every
tree whose fruit yields seed; to you it shall be for food.
Also, to every beast of the earth, to every bird of the air,
and to everything that creeps on the earth, in which there
is life, I have given every green herb for food"; and it was
so. (Genesis 1:29, 30)

God gave Adam his assignment plus the prepared abundant resources needed for Adam's living and assignment and added a bonus- a beautiful wife.

2. When the Beasts Go Marching In

And God said to Noah, "The end of all flesh has come
before Me, for the earth is filled with violence through
them; and behold, I will destroy them with the earth.
Make yourself an ark of gopherwood; make rooms in the
ark...And of every living thing of all flesh you shall bring
two of every sort into the ark, to keep them alive with

you; they shall be male and female. Of the birds after their kind, of animals after their kind, and of every creeping thing of the earth after its kind, two of every kind will come to you to keep them alive. And you shall take for yourself of all food that is eaten, and you shall gather it to yourself; and it shall be food for you and for them."

(Genesis 6:13-15, 19-21)

Noah's assignment was to preserve life. He was to gather all the animals. the above passage tells us that God caused all the animals he needed to come to him. Just imagine Noah waking up one day and the lion was knocking at his door! Whatever God sends you to gather, He can send to you.

3. The Hidden Ram

Abraham's mission was to make a sacrifice. God tested him by telling him to kill his son, Isaac. Abraham went in obedience. By the time He got there and was about to kill his son, God called on him to stop because

He had already provided the ram. He hid it there on the mountain before Abraham arrived.

Then Abraham lifted his eyes and looked, and there behind him was a ram caught in a thicket by its horns. So Abraham went and took the ram, and offered it up for a burnt offering instead of his son. And Abraham called the name of the place, The-Lord-Will-Provide; as it is said to this day, "In the Mount of the Lord it shall be provided."
(Genesis 22:13, 14).

Before you get to the place of your assignment, God has already hidden the provision needed.

4. 40 years of Miracles

Moses had a difficult task. He was sent by God to take a bunch of whinny, easily discouraged people through the wilderness to the Promised Land. He had to feed them, give them water, protect them and provide for all their physical needs for 40 years. The whole nation was unemployed for this whole period.

What do we see about God's provisions for assignments here? We see God miraculously supplying all that was needed. Food rained from heaven, water came from the rock, winds blew meat into the camp and the pillars of cloud and fire provided the air conditioning, direction and protection. They were amply supplied.

Now a wind went out from the Lord, and it brought quail from the sea and left them fluttering near the camp, about a day's journey on this side and about a day's journey on the other side, all around the camp, and about two cubits above the surface of the ground.

(Numbers 11:31)

5. Elijah is Fed

The stingy raven feeds Elijah and a widow woman meets his needs.

Then the word of the Lord came to him, saying, "Get away from here and turn eastward, and hide by the Brook Cherith, which flows into the Jordan. And it will be that you shall drink from the brook, and I have commanded the ravens to feed you there." So he went and did according to the word of the Lord, for he went and stayed by the Brook Cherith, which flows into the Jordan. The ravens brought him bread and meat in the morning, and bread and meat in the evening; and he drank from the brook. And it happened after a while that the brook dried up, because there had been no rain in the land. Then the word of the Lord came to him, saying, "Arise, go to Zarephath, which belongs to Sidon, and dwell there. See, I have commanded a widow there to provide for you." (1 Kings 17:2-9)

6. The Real Goldfish

Peter and Jesus' were paid with money from the fish's mouth.

Nevertheless, lest we offend them, go to the sea, cast in a hook, and take the fish that comes up first. And when you have opened its mouth, you will find a piece of money; take that and give it to them for Me and you." (Matthew 17:27)

7. The Disciples Sent Out with Nothing

And He said to them, "When I sent you without money bag, knapsack, and sandals, did you lack anything?" So they said, "Nothing." (Luke 22:35)

8. Paul's Needs Met

The Philippian church were Paul's ministry partners.

But I rejoiced in the Lord greatly that now at last your care for me has flourished again; though you surely did care, but you lacked opportunity.

Now you Philippians know also that in the beginning of the gospel, when I departed from Macedonia, no church shared with me concerning giving and receiving but you only. For even in Thessalonica you sent aid once and again for my necessities. Not that I seek the gift, but I seek the fruit that abounds to your account. Indeed I have all and abound. I am full, having received from Epaphroditus the things sent from you, a sweet-smelling aroma, an acceptable sacrifice, well pleasing to God. And my God shall supply all your need according to His riches in glory by Christ Jesus. (Philippians 4:10, 15-19)

I don't know about you but whenever I meditate on scriptures like these, I get excited knowing that God provides for everyone He sends. I know there will be times when you wonder where the supplies will come from and times when you have to take some steps of obedience to lay hold of the supplies.

There will times when you have to learn to work with what you have and be content but God has proved over and over that He always bills His will when we cooperate with Him. Like Hudson Taylor's motto says, "God's word done God's way will never lack His supplies."

COOPERATING WITH GOD

In the passages we just went through, you will notice that the people in the stories had to do something to lay hold on God's prepared provisions. In the provision of the quails, God could have dropped the quails right in the camp of the Israelites or even blow them into their tents, but He chose not to.

Instead He dropped them around the camp at a distance equivalent to a day's journey. So even though God had provided, the children of Israel would still have to walk a whole day to get the quail and another day to walk back to the camp.

In doing this, God is trying to show us that there is always man's part to His divine provisions. Supplies will never drop on you like ripe cherries off a tree. You will still have to do something to get it in. So what are your responsibilities as a missionary in receiving God's supplies?

PILLARS OF SUPERNATURAL SUPPLIES: MAN'S RESPONSIBILITY IN RECEIVING PROVISION

PILLAR 1: PRAYER AND FAITH

As I mentioned before in the chapter on rules of engagement, faith is indispensable in every issue of life and ministry. It is how we access divine supplies and transfer them from the spiritual world into the earth realm. When faith and prayer combine together, results are inevitable.

The stories of men of faith move me greatly. It inspires me when I see or hear of people who dared to believe God for things and stood steadfast until they received the answer. I am even more impressed if believing God and getting result is a pattern in their lives. Two of such men are Hudson Taylor and George Mueller. These two men were men of great faith.

Hudson Taylor was an English missionary to China who founded the China Inland Mission. He spent 51 years in China, raising up over 20 mission stations with more than 800 missionaries and establishing a Chinese church of 125,000 people with 35,000 of his own converts, baptizing 50,000 of them!

Shortly after he first moved to China, his mission board informed him that they couldn't send support to him again. He at first was disillusioned but he began to believe God for resources. He would ask God alone for supplies, without talking to anyone and supplies will come in miraculous ways. This is what eventually became what is called faith mission, where a missionary will only pray concerning financial needs and not inform anyone about it. By the time of his death, he had raised over 4 million dollars for the mission.

George Mueller was of another man of faith who in caring for thousands of orphans, raised purely by faith without soliciting support from anyone, an estimated amount of about 150 million dollars in today's currency.

How did they do it? Can we repeat the same? I say yes. By exercising faith in God like they did, we can also tap into the unlimited resources of heaven.

A Heavenly Grant

For this reason I am telling you, whatever you ask for in prayer, believe (trust and be confident) that it is granted to you, and you will [get it]. (Mark 11:24 AMP)

And when that time comes, you will ask nothing of Me
[you will need to ask Me no questions]. I assure you, most
solemnly I tell you, that My Father will grant you
whatever you ask in My Name [as presenting all that I
AM]. (John 16:23 AMP)

Notice the word "grant" in both of these passages. Jesus is telling us that God will respond to our prayer of faith by giving us a grant, a heavenly grant. One of the meanings of a grant is a sum of money given to a person or organization for a particular purpose.

In the United States, we have several government, foundational or corporate grants given for the purpose of doing some kinds of charity work or educational purposes. Many organizations hire grant writers to write proposals to the government and other foundations seeking grants for their work.

Jesus is telling us here that by asking in faith in His name, we have the privilege of receiving heavenly grants from the Father. To receive the grant for your ministry regularly, you will need to follow the instruction of Jesus in these passages. Let's parse the passages.

Whatever you ask for

This means that you must have something specific to ask. The way we have practiced this is to have a specific amount for a specific time period, say weekly, monthly or annually that we request a heavenly grant for in prayer. To determine this specific amount, you will need to calculate the total expense of your mission, including your personal expenses and that of every employee or staff working with you, if any.

After coming up with the total amount, determine how regularly you will need this amount to come in. For instance, it could be $10,000 a month or $2,000 a week or $ 120,000 a year. Be very specific. If this is the first time you are doing this, don't start with an amount so huge that you know you will not be able to wrap your faith around it. You don't start climbing at the top rung of the ladder.

In prayer

This type of prayer to request a grant is called a prayer of petition. The dictionary defines a petition as:

a. A solemn supplication or request to a superior authority; an entreaty.

b. A formal written document requesting a right or benefit from a person or group in authority.

So there is some formality and solemnity attached to making a petition. The practical way we have used is to write out a formal request for the grant. The following is an example of a petition we have used, some parts of it courtesy of Kenneth Copeland Ministries.

Sample Heavenly Petition

Be it known this day that on _____ _____, 2011, _____ pm, We prayed according to Mark 11;25 and received a heavenly grant of resources to cover the following needs in our lives and ministries. Father in the name of Jesus, We come boldly to the throne of grace to thank you for granting us our request according to your covenant promises in your unfailing word.

John 16:23 (Amplified) Jesus said, "I assure you, most solemnly I tell you, that my father will grant whatever you ask in my name. Jesus said in Mark 11:24 " Whatever you ask for in prayer, believe trust and be confident that it is granted you and you, and you will get it."

Your words states in Luke 6:38. "Give and it shall be given unto you: good measure, pressed down, and shaken together and running over shall men give to your bosom." In accordance with your covenant we give, CityLight gives. We sow seeds and so we thank you that this spiritual law is working on our behalf now.

Also according to Philippians 4:19, your word states," my God shall supply all your need according to his riches in glory by Christ Jesus. So we thank you that these needs have been supplied according to your heavenly supplies. According to 2 Corinthians 9:8, you have made all the earthly favors, relationships, wisdom, events and blessings necessary for these needs to be met, available and they are ours now. Thank you.

According to Mathew 18:18, We bind you Satan and all your forces and we render you helpless and unable to operate in Jesus name. You will not hinder our grant.

According to Hebrews 1:13, 14, and Mathew 26:52,53 we lose the legions of ministering spirits, enforcers of our covenant and in the name of Jesus, we charge them to go forth and cause our grant to come into our lives.

According to Genesis 1:28, We exercise authority over you the finances, properties and other material resources of the earth necessary for this grant and command you to come to us.

The grant is for the following:

1.

2.

3.

As it is written, Jeremiah 32:27 " Behold, I am the LORD, the God of all flesh: is there any thing too hard for me?" and " all things are possible to him that believeth. We believe.

Also Jesus you said in Mathew 18:19, "again I say unto you, that if two of you shall agree on earth as touching anything that they shall ask, it shall be done for them of my father which is in heaven."

Therefore _____ and I set ourselves in agreement, and we believe we receive now, and we praise you for it.

Have the specific needs of your mission written down alongside a few scriptures promising provisions. Read these scriptures to yourself regularly, believing them, then pray them out as a petition to God asking Him for the amounts you need. You could also join in agreement with another believer based on Matthew 18:19.

The plan is to pray this petition regularly and adjust the amounts as your needs change.

Believe (trust and be confident) that it is granted to you

Notice that the tenses of the petition are in the past. We are declaring that we received the grant when we asked and now we are just thanking God and keeping ourselves focused on His promise as we wait expectantly in faith for the physical manifestation. Doing this is like setting your thermostat of faith to a level and letting the supernatural forces of God go into motion to raise your financial temperature to this set level. It works!

You will get it

Getting it usually comes as a result of a plan that the Holy Spirit communicates to you as you stand in faith. He may tell you to take offerings, sell something, tell someone, conduct a fundraising drive, enlist partners or give something.

Remember God will not drop the quails in your camp. You will have to do something to go and gather them in. However, whatever you do, never put pressure on people or look to people as your source, keep your eyes on God and put pressure on His promises alone. This leads us to the next pillar of supplies, generosity.

PILLAR 2: GENEROSITY

There is one who scatters, yet increases more; And there is one who withholds more than is right, But it leads to poverty. The generous soul will be made rich, And he who waters will also be watered himself. (Proverbs 11:24, 25)

When you refresh others, you will also be refreshed. You must add this to the principle of faith. Something must be going out to others from your life and ministry for you to be entitled to resources. There is a principle of reciprocity that Jesus spoke about in the following passage.

"Judge not, and you shall not be judged. Condemn not, and you shall not be condemned. Forgive, and you will be forgiven. Give, and it will be given to you: good measure, pressed down, shaken together, and running over will be put into your bosom. For with the same measure that you use, it will be measured back to you." (Luke 6:37, 38)

He is saying that whatever proceeds out of you, whether judgment, condemnation, forgiveness or any other gifts or input into others will come back to you in multiplied form using the same standard or measure you use. This is a broad encompassing principle of life but I narrow it down to resources for missions here.

Whatever you make happen for others, God will make happen for you. Let your ministry be a giving ministry. Be a giver personally. Seek out other people and missions and invest some parts of what God has blessed you with already. This could be your money, time, skill or talent.

Don't be self-focused. The passage above reads like this in the message translation,

The world of the generous gets larger and larger; the world of the stingy gets smaller and smaller. The one who blesses others is abundantly blessed; those who help others are helped. (Proverbs 11:24, 25 MSG)

So if you want your world to grow larger and larger, then you must be generous. Generosity releases the grace of God that opens up unlimited supplies to the generous.

[Remember] this: he who sows sparingly and grudgingly will also reap sparingly and grudgingly, and he who sows generously [that blessings may come to someone] will also reap generously and with blessings. Let each one [give] as he has made up his own mind and purposed in his heart, not reluctantly or sorrowfully or under compulsion, for God loves (He takes pleasure in prizes above other things, and is unwilling to abandon or to do without) a cheerful (joyous, "prompt to do it") giver [whose heart is in his giving].

And God is able to make all grace (every favor and earthly blessing) come to you in abundance, so that you may always and under all circumstances and whatever the need be self-sufficient [possessing enough to require no aid or support and furnished in abundance for every good work and charitable donation]. As it is written, He [the benevolent person] scatters abroad; He gives to the poor; His deeds of justice and goodness and kindness and benevolence will go on and endure forever! And [God] Who provides seed for the sower and bread for eating will also provide and multiply your [resources for] sowing and increase the fruits of your righteousness [which manifests itself in active goodness, kindness, and charity]. Thus you will be enriched in all things and in every way, so that you can be generous, and [your generosity as it is] administered by us will bring forth thanksgiving to God.
(2 Corinthians 9:6-11 AMP)

Tithing and Partnership

A major way of practicing generosity is tithing. Tithing is giving ten percent of your intake to God. Be a personal tither to your church. In addition, let your ministry or businesses also tithe. Ask God to show you other ministries that you should tithe into. It might be a single ministry or several.

Specifically focus on ministries that have something that you desire to have in your mission; those that are bringing life to people, helping the poor and that have proven integrity. When you partner with other blessed ministries, you connect to the blessing and grace operating in them and you become a sharer of the grace on them. When you bless the blessed, you are blessed by God.

Yet it is beyond all contradiction that it is the lesser person who is blessed by the greater one. (Hebrews 7:7 AMP)

I will bless those who bless you, And I will curse him who curses you; And in you all the families of the earth shall be blessed." (Genesis 12:3)

Spiritual Impact

Another way of adding input into the lives of others is through spiritual impact. When people are touched spiritually through your ministry, their hearts are opened to support you financially and materially. Paul told the Romans,

If we have sown spiritual things for you, is it a great thing if we reap your material things? (1 Corinthians 9:11)

Jesus, when sending his disciples out on their first mission told them,

Carry neither money bag, knapsack, nor sandals; and greet no one along the road. But whatever house you enter, first say, 'Peace to this house.' And if a son of peace is there, your peace will rest on it; if not, it will return to you. And remain in the same house, eating and drinking such things as they give, for the laborer is worthy of his wages. Do not go from house to house. Whatever city you enter, and they receive you, eat such things as are set

187

before you. And heal the sick there, and say to them, 'The
kingdom of God has come near to you.' (Luke 10:4-9)

The disciples were to focus on spiritual impact on
the people they were sent to while God focused on
supplying their needs through the people they were
ministering to. It worked. Later Jesus asked them,

And He said to them, "When I sent you without money
bag, knapsack, and sandals, did you lack anything?" So
they said, "Nothing." (Luke 22:35)

All their needs were met. Spiritual impact will
always generate material returns. Those who are
transformed through your assignment are people that
God can potentially use to sustain you and your ministry
in the future.

It is like the case of the man that Joseph
interpreted a dream for who later recommended him to
Pharaoh. Spiritual impact is a seed, so develop yourself
and minister to people compassionately. Be careful
however, that money never becomes the motive of your

ministry to people. That is filthy lucre and it is not of God.

PILLAR 3: FRIEND RAISING

"And I say to you, make friends for yourselves by unrighteous mammon, that when you fail, they may receive you into an everlasting home. (Luke 16:9)

The third pillar of supernatural supplies is friend raising. Friend raising, a term popularized by Betty Barnett in her great book, Friend Raising: Building a Missionary Support Team that Lasts, is the practice of building authentic relationships with a view to raising a financial support team for mission work.[5] This is also called partner raising.

Many people do fundraising instead of friends raising. Never make raising money your focus, raise people. When you raise people, you automatically raise money. An African proverb says, "People are your clothes."

I always marvel when I read the story in Luke 5 of friends who brought in the paralyzed man to Jesus by breaking down the roof. I ask myself if there are people who will dare to break down the roof for me to get me to Jesus when I need their help. Everyone needs such friends.

Friend raising is the act of building lasting relationships with people who can carry your ministry. These kinds of relationships don't just happen, they are built.

This practice stems from the fact that support flows better in the context of relationships. This is scriptural. We see Jesus' ministry being supported by His friends.

Now it came to pass, afterward, that He went through every city and village, preaching and bringing the glad tidings of the kingdom of God. And the twelve were with Him, and certain women who had been healed of evil spirits and infirmities—Mary called Magdalene, out of whom had come seven demons, and Joanna the wife of Chuza, Herod's steward, and Susanna, and many others who provided for Him from their substance. (Luke 8:1-3)

Levi gave a large dinner at his home for Jesus. Everybody was there, tax men and other disreputable characters as guests at the dinner. (Luke 5:29 MSG)

The Philippian churches were friends and partners of Paul. They supported His ministry. He said to them,

I thank my God upon every remembrance of you, always in every prayer of mine making request for you all with joy, for your fellowship in the gospel from the first day until now. (Philippians 1:3-5)

Now you Philippians know also that in the beginning of the gospel, when I departed from Macedonia, no church shared with me concerning giving and receiving but you only. For even in Thessalonica you sent aid once and again for my necessities. (Philippians 4:15, 16).

191

So this is a scriptural practice that you can adopt in your mission. You will execute this practically by genuinely building great friendships and relationships with individuals and organizations.

In my book, *The 31 Immutable Laws of Relationships*, I outlined several principles of building lasting friendships. Three of the principles govern the initiation of relationships. Here is a summary of these principles.

> a. Orchestration principle: God arranges divine relationships so pray for them to come. Eve came to Adam, Barnabas came to Paul, Jesus went to Peter. Pray specifically to meet the people you need and people that need you.

> b. Conversion principle: Enemies and strangers are what friends are made of. (Hebrews 13:1). Sometimes when the people come your way, they may not look like friends initially. Learn to convert everything.

c. Intentionality principle: Acquaintances may be accidental but relationships are made and built intentionally. He that will have many friends must show himself friendly.

Initiate great relationships by applying these principles. Another great book that can help you in this area is the classic, *How to Win Friends and Influence People* by Dale Carnegie.

Practical Steps to Raising Friends

1. Start with what you have. Know that for everything you plan to do, you already have what it takes to start. So make a list of people in your current circle (family, friends, acquaintances, mentors, members of your church , friends, colleagues etc) that you feel could potentially be friends and partners of your mission.

2. If your ministry has events that people attend or you provide services or sell products, ask politely for your patrons' names and information.

3. Start praying for the people on this list. Ask God to open their hearts to a deeper relationship with you and your mission.

4. Initiate further interactions with them. Call, email or link up with them using the many social network platforms available to you.

5. Make genuine connections. Show genuine interest and support. Learn to listen to people about the most important topic to them: "themselves". Build bridges not walls.

6. Serve them in ways you can. Invest into their lives and missions. Being there for people takes you to another level in your relationships with them. If you stand with people, God will raise people to stand with you.

7. Don't manipulate people. People can sense if you are not genuine. Your goal is to build relationships with all even those who may not support you. Sow seeds

of relationships. You will not necessarily reap from the people you sow into but you will reap what you sow.

Do not be deceived, God is not mocked; for whatever a man sows, that he will also reap...And let us not grow weary while doing good, for in due season we shall reap if we do not lose heart. Therefore, as we have opportunity, let us do good to all, especially to those who are of the household of faith. (Galatians 6:7, 9, 10)

This leads to the final pillar of supernatural supplies, communication.

4. COMMUNICATION

And Moses spoke to all the congregation of the children of Israel, saying, "This is the thing which the Lord commanded, saying: 'Take from among you an offering to the Lord. Whoever is of a willing heart, let him bring it as an offering to the Lord: gold, silver, and bronze; (Exodus 35:4)

And all the congregation of the children of Israel departed from the presence of Moses. Then everyone came whose

195

heart was stirred, and everyone whose spirit was willing, and they brought the Lord's offering for the work of the tabernacle of meeting, for all its service, and for the holy garments. (Exodus 35:20, 21)

Communication in mission funding enables people to know the resources needed for the mission and gives people the opportunity to be part of it. It is not the same thing as begging. It is presenting to the friends you have raised, the vision God has given you so that they may have an opportunity to be a part of making it happen and reaping the rewards along with you.

If you don't give people the opportunity to know what you are doing, they will not be able to support it. You will be like a person winking in the dark. You know what you are doing but no one else knows. Great communication opens up the hearts of people to support your mission. Whatever people are not aware of cannot move their hearts. Jesus said,

"You are the light of the world. A city that is set on a hill cannot be hidden. Nor do they light a lamp and put it under a basket, but on a lampstand, and it gives light to all who re in the house. Let your light so shine before men, that they may see your good works and glorify your Father in heaven. (Matthew 5:14-16)

God wants us to communicate what we are doing to as many people as possible. There are people all around your city and nation who are dreaming of doing what you are doing or who would love to be a part of it financially if only they knew about it. Adequate communication will help you reach these people.

Practical Tips on Communication:

1. Use excellent written materials. People respect what is written and not just what you say. Use magazines, letters etc. You could set up a regular newsletter to mail to friends that contains your vision, its needs, its impact such as testimonies of people touched and more.

2. Use technology and social media platforms (videos, blogs, Facebook, twitter, email etc)

3. Organize informational events, such as banquets, partners' dinners etc.

4. Write grant requests to foundations and corporate organizations that have programs to support what you are doing. This is especially relevant in the United States where billions of dollars move from these organizations to great causes each year for various reasons including tax benefits. Nehemiah took advantage of such opportunities to fund his mission.

Furthermore I said to the king, "If it pleases the king, let letters be given to me for the governors of the region beyond the River, that they must permit me to pass through till I come to Judah, and a letter to Asaph the keeper of the king's forest, that he must give me timber to make beams for the gates of the citadel which pertains to the temple, for the city wall, and for the house that I will occupy." And the king granted them to me according to the good hand of my God upon me. Then I went to the governors in the region beyond the River, and gave them the king's letters. Now the king had sent captains of the army and horsemen with me. (Nehemiah 2:7-10)

5. Ask. Ask. Ask. Don't be afraid or ashamed to ask. You are not begging. You are not asking to consume it on yourself. You have a great cause from God. Destinies are depending on your doing what you are sent to do. Jesus was never ashamed to ask. Follow His example.

So it was, as the multitude pressed about Him to hear the word of God, that He stood by the Lake of Gennesaret, and saw two boats standing by the lake; but the fishermen had gone from them and were washing their nets. Then He got into one of the boats, which was Simon's, and asked him to put out a little from the land. And He sat down and taught the multitudes from the boat. (Luke 5:1-3)

And it came to pass, when He drew near to Bethphage and Bethany, at the mountain called Olivet, that He sent two of His disciples, saying, "Go into the village opposite you, where as you enter you will find a colt tied, on which no one has ever sat. Loose it and bring it here. And if anyone asks you, 'Why are you loosing it?' thus you shall say to him, 'Because the Lord has need of it.'" (Luke 19:29-31).

There are tons of resources the Lord has need of which are still in people's hand. They won't be released until someone asks.

If you will put these four pillars: faith, generosity, friend raising and communication in place, you will have taken the symbolic day journey to where God has provided the quails of supplies for your mission. You will start gathering in abundance to support you and your mission.

Finally, here are some extra cautions you need to take in funding your mission.

CAUTIONS IN MISSION FUNDING

1. Don't manipulate people for money. Never use people to get things, use things to serve people. Don't get involved in gimmicks to manipulate people.

2. Don't beg or borrow. The borrower is servant to the lender. Begging is putting your trust in man. God will take care of you. "I have been young, and now am old; Yet I have not seen the righteous forsaken, Nor his descendants begging bread."(Psalm 37:25)

3. Don't worry about resources. Cast your cares on Him. You didn't send yourself. If He sent you, He'll take care of His bills. *He who calls you is faithful, who also will do it.* (1 Thessalonians 5:24)

4. Have financial integrity. Have good records that are open to all. Account for every fund that comes in and goes out. Be transparent. Don't be the one exclusively in charge of the finances of your ministry. Manage the resources you have been given well. Be honest and accurate in your reports and communication of your needs. Don't exaggerate. Pay taxes. Separate your

personal finances from your ministry finances. Paul said,

"And we have sent with him the brother whose praise is in the gospel throughout all the churches, and not only that, but who was also chosen by the churches to travel with us with this gift, which is administered by us to the glory of the Lord Himself and to show your ready mind, avoiding this: that anyone should blame us in this lavish gift which is administered by us— providing honorable things, not only in the sight of the Lord, but also in the sight of men. (2 Corinthians 8:18-21)

5. Cultivate a consistent attitude of abundance. Refuse to have a poverty mentality. Even if you face a need, trust that you can carry out your mission by God's ability; that He will make a way somehow, even in tight situations. Never stop being generous.

"Not that I speak in regard to need, for I have learned in whatever state I am, to be content: I know how to be abased, and I know how to abound. Everywhere and in all things I have learned both to be full and to be hungry,

both to abound and to suffer need. I can do all things through Christ who strengthens me. (Philippians 4:11-13)

6. Be grateful. Thank God for what you have and genuinely appreciate the people who are supporting you.

7. Never let financial consideration be the basis of any service, relationship or ministry you provide. Yes, you will be compensated for your work but don't make it the basis of your mission.

Don't treat people honorable just because they have money or they give more. Don't sell your gifts or curry favors. God is your source not man. If you are a preacher, don't arrange meetings based on the honorarium you will receive. Go to where God sends you even if you will be given nothing.

"My brethren, do not hold the faith of our Lord Jesus Christ, the Lord of glory, with partiality. For if there should come into your assembly a man with gold rings, in fine apparel, and there should also come in a poor man in filthy clothes, and you pay attention to the one wearing

the fine clothes and say to him, "You sit here in a good place," and say to the poor man, "You stand there," or, "Sit here at my footstool," have you not shown partiality among yourselves, and become judges with evil thoughts?
(James 2:1-4)

I have coveted no one's silver or gold or apparel. Yes, you yourselves know that these hands have provided for my necessities, and for those who were with me. I have shown you in every way, by laboring like this, that you must support the weak. And remember the words of the Lord Jesus, that He said, 'It is more blessed to give than to receive.' " (Acts 20:33-35)

May you enjoy unlimited divine supplies in your mission as you practice these truths.

CHAPTER 8

MULTIPLYING MINISTRY IMPACT

By this My Father is glorified, that you bear much fruit; so you will be My disciples. (John 15:8)

I f you have invested a large part of your nest egg in, say Apple's stock, you treat any news about Apple much differently than someone who has no stake in the company. You desire that the company prospers and generates huge profits.

In the same way, God, having invested a lot in you, says it is His desire that His investments produce profits—lots of it. God wants to look at the income statement of His kingdom and see huge returns from the assignment He gave you.

The parable of the talent shows this investment-conscious side of God. When the master, which depicts God, came back to ask for what His servants did with the talents they were given, those who produced profits were commended while the only one who hid his was reprimanded and dispossessed of what He had.

"But his lord answered and said to him, 'You wicked and lazy servant, you knew that I reap where I have not sown, and gather where I have not scattered seed. So you ought to have deposited my money with the bankers, and at my coming I would have received back my own with interest. So take the talent from him, and give it to him who has ten talents. 'For to everyone who has, more will be given, and he will have abundance; but from him who does not have, even what he has will be taken away.

(Matthew 25:26-29)

MINISTRY IMPACT

God wants many profits from our lives. He wants you to produce multiplied results with whatever He has committed into your hands. He wants your mission to generate multiplied impact. It glorifies Him when you bear much fruit.

Ministry is meant to produce results. Every calling must make some sort of impact. A ministry without impact lacks credibility because impact is the accreditation of a mission from God. Results in ministry prove to others that God is with you.

This man came to Jesus by night and said to Him, "Rabbi, we know that You are a teacher come from God; for no one can do these signs that You do unless God is with him." (John 3:2)

FRUITLESSNESS IS UNACCEPTABLE

He also spoke this parable: "A certain man had a fig tree planted in his vineyard, and he came seeking fruit on it and found none. Then he said to the keeper of his vineyard, 'Look, for three years I have come seeking fruit on this fig tree and find none. Cut it down; why does it use up the ground?' But he answered and said to him, 'Sir, let it alone this year also, until I dig around it and fertilize it.

And if it bears fruit, well. But if not, after that you can cut it down.' " (Luke 13:6-9)

I tell people that according to this parable, there is a need to periodically assess the things you are doing. I understand that mission work, especially in some places might take years to bear fruits, but if you are doing anything for years and years on end and there is not one visible manifestation of fruit, it is either a sign that there is a need for assessment and a change of course, or it's a message that you need to get with God and find out what you need to do to produce results.

Fruitlessness or lack of results in your mission is equivalent to uselessness and it eventually leads to irrelevance. Jesus said: "Every tree that does not bear good fruit is cut down and thrown into the fire." (Matthew 7:19).

TYPES OF MINISTRY IMPACT

I have spent considerable time searching the scriptures for the mind of God regarding the specific types of impact He expects ministries to produce. I wanted to know what counts as a return for His investments as I pursue His assignment for my life. Here are the things I discovered from my studies.

1. Impact on People

God is in the people business. He loves people. He created the universe for people. He brought forth everything we see in nature for people. He established covenants with people to ensure a legal way of helping them every time. He sends His word to people. He raises up prophets deliverers, empowers and sends them to people. He came to the earth for people.

While He was on the earth, He went everywhere healing and delivering people. Then He went to the cross and died for people. Now He is in heaven as the high priest, interceding for people.

209

For God so loved the world that He gave His only begotten Son, that whoever believes in Him should not perish but have everlasting life. (John 3:16)

As I said at the beginning of this book, the purpose for every calling from God is to help people. Ministry is the intersection of the compassion of God flowing through a person and a particular need of people. So, one of the ways the impact of your assignment is judged is if people are being touched by it.

For we are His workmanship, created in Christ Jesus for good works, which God prepared beforehand that we should walk in them. (Ephesians 2:10)

God cares about people. That is one of the primary reasons why He called you- to be a carrier of His love to them. So, your ministry should be affecting people in some ways: leading them to Christ, meeting spiritual, emotional, physical or financial needs. God has sent you with some solutions to someone or a group of people. Jesus delineated the people that would be impacted by His mission from the beginning, fortunately, the list included all of us. His ministry was about people.

"The Spirit of the Lord is upon Me, Because He has anointed Me To preach the gospel to the poor; He has sent Me to heal the brokenhearted, To proclaim liberty to the captives And recovery of sight to the blind, To set at liberty those who are oppressed; (Luke 4:18)

These were categories of people. These were the beneficiaries of the calling and the anointing on Jesus. His ministry was validated by impact on people. When John the Baptist sent people to ask Him if He was the anointed one they had been expecting,

Jesus did not present a theological proof but results. He said, *" The blind see and the lame walk; the lepers are cleansed and the deaf hear; the dead are raised up and the poor have the gospel preached to them.* (Matthew 11:5). People were on His mind.

2. Impact on Places

Apart from people, God's assignment also impacts places. God sends people to particular locations to establish His will there. Phillip was sent to Samaria, Jonah to Nineveh. Joseph was sent to Egypt; Saint Patrick to Ireland, William Carey to India and David Livingstone to Africa.

God desires not just to impact the people of these places, but their living context itself. Jesus was sent to seek that which was lost on earth, not only the lost people, but to restore the lost earth back to God ultimately (Colossians 1:19-20).

3. Impact on Systems.

There are callings to change existing systems. An example is William Wilberforce's assignment to eradicate slavery. He wasn't sent directly to the slaves themselves but to the British legislature on behalf of the slaves. There are scientists whose callings are to invent things that will improve systems and politicians whose callings are to address systemic issues in a city or nation. For example, the impact of your calling could be to change the unjust economic system of an industry, reform the healthcare of a city or establish a new order in the educational system of a community.

4. Impact of Legacy

God aims primarily at creating legacies with some assignments. The real impacts of such callings usually transcend their lifetime into succeeding generations. An example is Abraham, whose calling was to create an opportunity for God to raise a family of people through which the Messiah will be born and to be an example of faith to those who will believe in God after him. (Genesis 12:1-3).

5. Impact on Heaven

Everyone who is called should make a heavenly impact. We are supposed to cause glory to ascend to God in our ministries. We are to give God pleasure and cause rejoicing in heaven as we populate heaven with new souls.

"I say to you that likewise there will be more joy in heaven over one sinner who repents than over ninety-nine just persons who need no repentance. (Luke 15:7)

6. Impact on Hell

We are all also called to make an impact on hell. The devil and his hosts must feel the impact of our missions and cringe. We and our missions should be known and feared in hell because we torment Satan and depopulate his illegitimate kingdom. Satan should heave a sigh of relief when we go to bed at night and should cry out in alarm when our eyes open to the day.

"And the evil spirit answered and said, "Jesus I know, and Paul I know; but who are you?" (Acts 19:15)

MOVING FROM LITTLE FRUIT TO MUCH FRUIT

Now that I've enumerated the kind of impact that God wants our ministries to have, I will now focus on how to multiply its impact, knowing that God is expecting much fruit from our lives.

1. Multiply your Impact by Multiplying His Influence in Your Life

Abide in Me, and I in you. As the branch cannot bear fruit

of itself, unless it abides in the vine, neither can you,

unless you abide in Me. "I am the vine, you are the

branches. He who abides in Me, and I in him, bears much

fruit; for without Me you can do nothing. (John 15:4, 5)

Jesus says, anyone who abides in Him will bear much fruit. Anyone who stays hooked up to Him will produce great results and generate multiplied impact. This is so because impact is a product of the anointing and the anointing is a byproduct of abiding in Christ.

"The Spirit of the Lord God is upon Me, Because the Lord

has anointed Me To preach good tidings to the poor; He

has sent Me to heal the brokenhearted, To proclaim

liberty to the captives, And the opening of the prison to

those who are bound; To proclaim the acceptable year of

the Lord, And the day of vengeance of our God; To
comfort all who mourn, To console those who mourn in
Zion, To give them beauty for ashes, The oil of joy for
mourning, The garment of praise for the spirit of
heaviness; That they may be called trees of righteousness,
The planting of the Lord, that He may be glorified." And
they shall rebuild the old ruins, They shall raise up the
former desolations, And they shall repair the ruined cities,
The desolations of many generations. (Isaiah 61:1-4)

If you look closely at these verses, you will notice that all the forms of impact that I listed earlier are in this scripture (people, places, systems, legacy, heaven and hell) and they are all precipitated because of the anointing.

The anointing is the force of multiplied impact. The more of it operating in your life, no matter the direction of your calling, the more impact you will make. Until the anointing came on Jesus at river Jordan and He was led into the wilderness, His ministry had no exploits. After He was anointed, it was written,

Then Jesus returned in the power of the Spirit to Galilee, and news of Him went out through all the surrounding region. (Luke 4:14).

The anointing announced His ministry and He began to do exploits. The anointing is not only for fiery preachers. It is for everyone on a mission. You can be anointed for business, politics and parenthood. You can be an anointed student, entertainer or scientist. The anointing is the divine ability given by God to carry out the assignments He has delegated.

The anointing brings impact. It was what was on Joseph, that helped him interpret dreams. It was the Spirit on Moses that gave him the ability to lead; it came on Joshua and gave him wisdom to conquer.

"Now Joshua the son of Nun was full of the spirit of wisdom, for Moses had laid his hands on him; so the children of Israel heeded him, and did as the Lord had commanded Moses.   (Deuteronomy 34:9).

It was on Solomon, Samson and Elijah producing feats of wisdom and power. It was what Elisha cried out to receive from Elijah.

And so it was, when they had crossed over, that Elijah said to Elisha, "Ask! What may I do for you, before I am taken away from you?" Elisha said, "Please let a double portion of your spirit be upon me." (2 Kings 2:9).

It was on the prophets, enabling them to see beyond their times. Daniel had it and he could interpret dreams and dissolve doubts. Before Jesus allowed His disciples to begin the work of ministry after His resurrection, He told them,

Behold, I send the Promise of My Father upon you; but tarry in the city of Jerusalem until you are endued with power from on high." (Luke 24:49)

To be endued is to be clothed. The anointing is a clothing of power from heaven. It is God on man, doing what only God can do. It came on the apostles on the day of Pentecost and they turned their worlds around. It was so strong on Peter that people came from surrounding cities and placed the sick on his pathway and were here healed just by the casting of his shadow. Paul had it so much that,

... God worked unusual miracles by the hands of Paul, so that even handkerchiefs or aprons were brought from his body to the sick, and the diseases left them and the evil spirits went out of them. (Acts 19:11, 12).

The anointing was the force behind all the ministries with great impact that we read and hear about: Wesley, Spurgeon, Moody, Finney, Wigglesworth, Seymour, Kathryn Kulman, Oral Roberts, Kenneth Hagin, Billy Graham.

It is the force propelling great apostles of God like David Oyedepo, Enoch Adeboye, Sam Adeyemi, Sunday Adelaja, Kenneth Copeland and many others.

The anointing is the Holy Spirit's influence on a person. This influence can be small or great or non-existent, so there are varying degrees of the anointing.

The greater the level of the anointing on you, the more impacts you can make. Therefore, in order to increase impact, seek an increase in the anointing. Increase in the anointing comes by abiding, staying hooked up to Him.

To abide is not to visit but to make Him your habitation. Jesus is not talking about you experiencing a touch of Him once in a while, He is speaking about dwelling in the secret place of His power and presence. This is where the divine sap for abundant fruitfulness flows unhindered into your life.

How to Abide

a. Do Away with Sin.

Behold, the Lord's hand is not shortened, That it cannot save; Nor His ear heavy, That it cannot hear. But your iniquities have separated you from your God; And your sins have hidden His face from you, So that He will not hear. (Isaiah 59:1, 2)

Sin separates us from Him. It creates a gap between us and God. It drains the anointing, clogs the expression of His power through us and hinders our fellowship with Him. The great thing is that God has dealt with our sins. He dealt with our inherited sin nature by becoming sin on the cross and exchanged His righteousness with us. Then He dealt with our acts of sin by shedding His blood on the cross.

This shed blood offers forgiveness and restoration to fellowship (staying hooked) if we confess our sins to Him.

If we say that we have fellowship with Him, and walk in darkness, we lie and do not practice the truth. But if we walk in the light as He is in the light, we have fellowship with one another, and the blood of Jesus Christ His Son cleanses us from all sin. If we say that we have no sin, we deceive ourselves, and the truth is not in us. If we confess our sins, He is faithful and just to forgive us our sins and to cleanse us from all unrighteousness. (1 John 1:6-9).

The way to deal with the practice of sin is to confess and renounce it.

He who covers his sins will not prosper, But whoever confesses and forsakes them will have mercy.
(Proverbs 28:13)

If you want to walk in the anointing of God, then you must get rid of any known sins in your life by confessing them to God and forsaking them.

You have loved righteousness and hated lawlessness; Therefore God, Your God, has anointed You With the oil of gladness more than Your companions."
(Hebrews 1:9 NKJV)

b. Invest Time with God Consistently.

Time spent with God studying, meditating and listening to His word, praying and seeking Him will multiply the anointing on your life and consequently your impact in ministry. This happens because in His presence we are changed. He rubs off on us and the ointment He pours on us is the anointing. As we are changed as vessels, He is able to pour more of His wine into our lives since new wine requires new vessels.

Pruning

Every branch in Me that does not bear fruit He takes away; and every branch that bears fruit He prunes, that it may bear more fruit. (John 15:2)

Pruning is the selective removal of diseased, damaged, dead, non- productive, structurally unsound, or otherwise unwanted tissue from plants. God does this to us in His presence. The less of those dead hanging weights we have in our lives, the more fruits we are able to bear.

I learned from Pastor Sunday Adelaja that he has the habit of separating himself from everything for one week out of each month to be with God. I have broken into new dimensions of the anointing by even a limited practice of this. Every time I take time out to be with God for extended periods of time, I notice an increase in God's power and wisdom flowing through my life.

223

On one occasion, I had separated myself for days of fasting and praying. When I returned back to church, I could see the healing anointing of God flowing in my life at a higher dimension with healings of various diseases including deafness and blindness in people.

c. Walk in Love

And we have known and believed the love that God has for us. God is love, and he who abides in love abides in God, and God in him. (1 John 4:16)

So one of the ways of staying hooked to Him in order to produce much fruit, is to ensure that you are practicing the love of God. Unforgiveness and strife chokes the anointing. Avoid them. As you do these consistently, the influence of God will pervade your life, thereby multiplying your results.

2. Multiply Your Impact by Daring to Do

Most assuredly, I say to you, unless a grain of wheat falls into the ground and dies, it remains alone; but if it dies, it produces much grain. (John 12:24)

Meditating on this verse, I could see in my mind, a grain of wheat hanging to the wheat plant, not wanting to fall off to the ground, but becoming rotten and literally dying as it goes through the process of bringing forth new life.

I could see in my mind times that I felt more comfortable with the status quo when God was calling me to detach myself because He had something greater in store—times that fear will grip me when He tells me to do something different, give some more, go to a new place, or begin a new ministry initiative.

We all go through that but until we take those new steps, we will remain limited in results, remaining alone like the single grain but if we go ahead and obey, even though it stretches us or temporarily inconveniences us, we will eventually get to a point where our fruits will be much.

So what steps is He asking you to take that looks impossible? What path is He pointing you to that looks narrow and difficult? What is He asking you to give that is hard to let go of? Trust Him for grace to obey. At the end of the path is increased fruitfulness.

3. Multiply Your Impact by Multiplying Yourself

And the things that you have heard from me among many witnesses, commit these to faithful men who will be able to teach others also. (2 Timothy 2:2)

Paul wrote this to Timothy, his spiritual son. It was an instruction showing him how to multiply his impact. He was to commit what he had learned from Paul to others who will then do the same to others and thus continue a chain that continues on and on, multiplying to many. This is wisdom.

If you want to multiply the impact of your mission, create opportunities for others to do what you do by multiplying yourself in them through discipleship or apprenticeship. Don't hoard the things that God has taught you, pass them on to others. Implant your vision in other people. Show them how you do what you do.

This is what Jesus did with His twelve disciples. He spent three years with them, teaching them and letting them see how He functioned. He delegated things to them, allowed them to make mistakes and stepped in when they couldn't do some things like healing a demon possessed man.

However, after He left the scene, those men took what they had learned by hearing and watching Him and multiplied the impact of His gospel all over the world. We are still being impacted through their writings.

Publications and Media

Another way to multiply the impact of your ministry by is through the use of written materials.

Written materials can go to places you may be unable to go. Johannes Gutenberg, the inventor of the printing press said: "Let us break the seal which seals up holy things and give wings to Truth in order that she may win every soul that comes into the world by her word, no longer written at great expense by hands easily palsied, but multiplied like the wind by an untiring machine."

He was saying that books have the ability to impart knowledge, influence nations, transcend geography, transform lives and even out-live their authors.

A book is the author and his ideas packaged in a form that requires neither passport nor visa. It has no accent; hence, there is no limit to its reach if it is excellently packaged. It is the author being in a million or more places at the same time multiplying his effort and grace. No wonder, God chose to reveal Himself, in a book, the bible.

The media has the same multiplying effect. The impact of your ministry can extend to places and even continue after your life, through the many available mediums of communication that are present now. Make use of them as God leads you.

4. Multiply Your Impact Through Partnership

A story in the Old Testament brings out a very important truth about partnership. David and some of his men had just returned from a successful battle to save their captured family members from the Amalekites. They came back with a large spoil from the battle to meet some other men who had stayed behind to watch their supplies.

"Now David came to the two hundred men who had been so weary that they could not follow David, whom they also had made to stay at the Brook Besor. So they went out to meet David and to meet the people who were with him. And when David came near the people, he greeted them. Then all the wicked and worthless men of those who went

*with David answered and said, "Because they did not go
with us, we will not give them any of the spoil that we
have recovered, except for every man's wife and children,
that they may lead them away and depart."*

*But David said, "My brethren, you shall not do so with
what the Lord has given us, who has preserved us and
delivered into our hand the troop that came against us.
For who will heed you in this matter? But as his part is
who goes down to the battle, so shall his part be who stays
by the supplies; they shall share alike. So it was, from that
day forward; he made it a statute and an ordinance for
Israel to this day."   (1 Samuel 30: 21-25)*

This is a principle of partnership. Everyone who is part of the collaboration enjoys the same reward no matter the type of role they played. The results of the partnership are shared by all.

Thus, rather than settling down to results achievable by the capability of one, everyone enjoys results produced by the combination of all who are in partnership. It is like individual drops of water from the rain combining together to become a very powerful flood that can sweep strongly erected houses and tall trees away. On its own, a drop of water can move almost nothing, but when it is joined together with other drops, its capacity to move things multiplies.

The same effort you are exerting now can produce greater impact if you join up with others. This is the reason why one of the goals of the devil is to keep the body of Christ divided.

A city could have several churches but each one like a drop of water on its own, keeps to itself and defends its turf. It feels like it is powerful and can move things on its own but imagine what could happen if the churches collaborated together. A mighty stream of God would emerge to make the needed impact on the city.

I experienced this power of partnership recently during an annual event we organize in our community in Chicago called LightFest. It is an event in which members of our church will set up open air games, free food, invite people from the community, perform acts of service which we call "acts of random kindness", pray and evangelize the community.

Before the most recent ones, we used the go-it-alone method. The church organized and paid for everything and then invited people in the community to join us. At best, our results were minimal using this method.

However, in the most recent ones, we decided to partner with organizations in the community who organized similar events. So rather than each group doing their thing, we all collaborated together to do just one event. The result was phenomenal, far exceeding what either of us had ever achieved in the past when we were on our own. More people were touched, more lives were touched and more activities to engage the community were made possible by the partnership. We also discovered that teaming up with others cost us much less than we usually spent on the event in the past which had fewer results.

Partnership multiplies efforts and reduces the weight on those who are part of the arrangement. It is very heavy for one individual alone to carry a really heavy table, but when other people join in, the work becomes a breeze. Collaborate with others for greater impact.

CHAPTER 9

KEEP THE END IN MIND

"So teach us to number our days, That we may gain a heart of wisdom." (Psalm 90:12)

There is a cemetery not too far from my former home that I drove past on many occasions. Those few minutes of seeing the array of tombstones were usually very sobering. There is something about the graveyard that brings a proper perspective to life. You could see from the road the inscriptions on some of the graves.

Each grave has a beginning and an ending date inscribed on it with a dash in between. The dates tell of life's beginning and conclusion. The dash also has a philosophical meaning. It represents the sum total of the existence of the departed, their biographies, comprising of pains, joys, accomplishment, opportunities used or lost, and most importantly, their preparedness or lack thereof for eternity.The beginning date of birth was the entrance into time, a brief interlude out of eternity and the ending date is the exit from time back into eternity. The dash is the opportunity of life. The following are some other messages the graveyard sends to us.

LIFE IS FINITE

The grave yard reminds that life is a finite asset. It is sobering to say, but you are gradually wrapping up in life. Like it goes for the cycle of the day, there is a morning, afternoon and night of life. In the morning, life buds like the flower in spring, in the evening it withers. You are either in the morning, afternoon, dusk or evening of life. Each life season has its opportunities that must be maximized or they may be lost forever.

King Solomon admonishes in the wisdom book that you should,

Honor and enjoy your Creator while you're still young,
Before the years take their toll and your vigor wanes,
Before your vision dims and the world blurs. And the
winter years keep you close to the fire. In old age, your
body no longer serves you so well. Muscles slacken, grip
weakens, joints stiffen. The shades are pulled down on the
world. You can't come and go at will. Things grind to a
halt. The hum of the household fades away. You are
wakened now by bird-song. Hikes to the mountains are a
thing of the past. Even a stroll down the road has its
terrors. Your hair turns apple-blossom white, Adorning a
fragile and impotent matchstick body. Yes, you're well on
your way to eternal rest, While your friends make plans
for your funeral. Life, lovely while it lasts, is soon over. Life
as we know it, precious and beautiful, ends. The body is
put back in the same ground it came from. The spirit
returns to God, who first breathed it.
(Ecclesiastes 12:1-7 MSG)

You should never live without the constant
awareness that your life in its present form will not last
forever, endeavoring to make use of every opportunity

the season presents you to pursue your mission before life's conclusion.

LIFE IS BRIEF

It also reminds that life is brief. While finitude has to do with the reality that it has an ending, the brevity of life speak to how short a time it is we have on earth. James says,

Come now, you who say, "Today or tomorrow we will go to such and such a city, spend a year there, buy and sell, and make a profit"; whereas you do not know what will happen tomorrow. For what is your life? It is even a vapor that appears for a little time and then vanishes away. (James 4:13, 14)

Even with the advances in medicine, most individual's life expectancy is at most a few decades. Even if you live up to a century or more, compared to eternity, this is still just a blip. That is all the opportunity you have to do all that you have been assigned to do in our earthly sojourn.

Just look back now at the years that have elapsed in your life. Doesn't it seem like yesterday that you were a child, or graduated, got married or were a teenager. The brevity of life means you cannot afford to squander life away on frivolities. It is short and must be put to its intended use, which is to fulfill your assignment.

LIFE IS MEASURABLE

One other lesson from the graveyard is the measurability of life. The dates on each grave are measurements. They represents time. They encapsulate the seconds, minutes, hours, months, days, weeks and years that the individual used on the earth.

Measurability is a necessary ingredient for proper planning. It makes it possible to divide life into discrete chunks that can have values, use, goals and results attached to them. In other words, it is possible to divide the accomplishment of certain goals and purpose in life into smaller chunks that eventually culminate in the full accomplishment of your overall purpose. The psalmist calls this numbering your days, assigning purposes to each time unit of life with a view of the end. *"So teach us to number our days, That we may gain a heart of wisdom."* (Psalm 90:12)

LIFE MUST BE EMPTIED

Also, the graveyard is a place of wealth. Dr. Myles Munroe said in one of his messages on potentials that the wealthiest place on earth is not the oil fields of the middle east, nor the diamond mines of South Africa, but the graveyard.

Why? Because it is at the graveyard where unused potentials, unfulfilled missions and untapped potentials lie wasted. The graveyard is a place of buried treasures; treasures that can never be utilized again — forever gone.

In view of this, we must make a commitment to die empty, that is, to leave this world knowing that every potential in us is tapped into; every purpose accomplished; every deed of love poured out on orders;

every talent utilized, until we are emptied out. We must make a commitment not to contribute to the wealth of the graveyard.

Paul the Apostle, in his last book, written to Timothy, inserted his valedictory, using a similar language to Dr. Munroe's,

"For I am already being poured out as a drink offering, and the time of my departure is at hand. I have fought the good fight, I have finished the race, I have kept the faith. Finally, there is laid up for me the crown of righteousness, which the Lord, the righteous Judge, will give to me on that Day, and not to me only but also to all who have loved His appearing. (2 Timothy 4:6-8)

Paul died empty. He finished his race, kept the faith and completed his mission. He did not quit by the wayside. He endured, following the one who called him fully to the end, and despite all the odds he faced, he fulfilled his mission. It should be our goals to have such a valedictory of fulfillment at the end of our lives.

LIFE IS NON-RENEWABLE

The grave yard also speaks of finality. You have only one life. There is no spare one as you would have a spare tire. Life once ended, cannot be relived. There are no do-overs. It is an opportunity that comes once and never comes again.

Granted, there will be a resurrection and a continuation of life in eternity, but that life is going to be based on how well you utilize the opportunity of the current life. The writer of the book of Hebrews says, "And as it is appointed for men to die once, but after this the judgment" (Hebrews 9:27).

The next life is a reward based on opportunity used now in this life. Your life in the current form is non-renewable. It is like the minutes you have on most mobile phone plans. You either use them or lose them. Once it is gone, it is gone forever. Therefore, to avoid regrets, reject all distractions and focus on finding and fulfilling your mission. Take the admonition of the following poem for which the exact author is unknown:

"I shall pass through this world but once! Any good thing, therefore, that I can do or any kindness that I can show to any human being, let me do it now, in his name, and for his sake! Let me not defer or neglect it, for I shall not pass this way again."

LIFE IS A STEWARDSHIP

Life is bestowed. It is never self-acquired. Someone gave it to you. The one who gave it to you is the real owner. The ultimate author of your life is God. He created you and gave you the breath of life. So, being the real owner, you owe him allegiance and you are accountable to him on how you utilize his asset.

Furthermore, he not only gave you life by authoring it, but in order to restore your diminished life as a result of your sin, he also gave his life for you on the cross when he died on your behalf (John 3:16). He died so you might life. There is therefore no doubt that you owe him your life. To bring this point home read the following true story.

> There is an old story about a man by the name of John Griffith, who lived in Oklahoma in 1929. He had lost all he had in the stock market crash. He moved to Mississippi where he took a job as a bridge operator for a railroad trestle. In 1937 he was involved in a horrible accident.

> One day his 8 year-old son, Greg, spent the day with his Dad at work. The boy poked around the office and asked dozens of questions - just like little boys do. The bridge was over a river and whenever a ship came John had to open the bridge to allow the ships to pass. The day the boy was there with his father a ship was coming so John opened up the draw bridge.

> After a moment or two he realized his son wasn't in the office and as he looked around, to his horror, John saw his son climbing around on the gears of the draw bridge. He hurried outside to rescue his son but just then he heard a fast approaching passenger train, the Memphis

Express, filled with 400 people. He yelled to his son, but the noise of the now clearing ship and the oncoming train made it impossible for the boy to hear him.

All of a sudden John Griffith realized his horrible dilemma. If he took the time to rescue his son, the train would crash, killing all aboard, but if he closed the bridge, the boy will be crushed in the gears. John would sacrifice his son. He made the horrible decision, pulled the lever and closed the bridge. It is said, as the train went by, John could see the faces of the passengers, some reading, some even waving, all of them oblivious to the sacrifice that had just been made for them. [6]

That's a great illustration of what God did for us. Now we must not be like the people on the train who were oblivious to the sacrifice of a son. We must show our gratitude by living our lives, knowing that it is a gift that came at a cost to God. We must be good stewards of life by maximizing every moment of it, fulfilling his assignment for us.

LIFE MUST BE LIVED WITH THE END IN MIND

Another message the graveyard conveys is that we must live life with the end in mind. On some graves, epitaphs are written summing up the lives of the individuals. These pithy sayings have the power to make a thinking person weep. Here are some powerful examples,

1. His courage, His smile, His grace gladdened the hearts of those who have had the privilege of loving Him.

2. Those we love remain with us for love itself lives on.

3. But O for the touch of a vanished hand and the sound of a voice that is still. -Tennyson

4. For they conquer who believe they can. -Virgil

5. An inspiration to all.

6. There was grace in her steps, love in every gesture.

7. Life is not forever. Love is.

8. May she be remembered as she remembered others.

246

9. Of tender heart and generous spirit.

10. Your patient courage is a beloved memory.

11. She graced her family with acts of loving kindness.

12. How beautiful life was to me.

13. Her works were kindness, her deeds were love.

14. Tender mother, a faithful friend.

15. A friend to many and sadly missed.

16. Our love is forever.

17. Wonderful was your love for us.

18. They gave their today for our tomorrow.

19. While we have time, let us do good.

20. Step softly, a dream lies buried here[7]

What does all this mean to you? One day you are going to have one written about you. What do you want it to say? Imagine your funeral, what are the people present going to say about you. How will your obituary read? Will it speak of unfulfilled dreams or a life of accomplishments? Will you be judged as loving or selfish? Godly or vain? What will your spouse say? What will your children, family, coworkers and community say? What legacy will you live behind?

Most importantly, what will God say? Will he say, welcome good and faithful servant or will he say. I never knew you? Now is the time to decide- time to maximize life by living with the end in mind - going after your assignment in life and giving it all you've got. Never forget that your mission is possible.

Meet the Greatest Person Alive!

I want to share with you about the most important decision that you can ever make in life. Jesus came to the earth to live and die, so that you might have life and live life abundantly, but the devil also has come to steal, kill and destroy. Winning or losing in life depends on whose lordship you are under; either Jesus or the devil. Romans 10:9 says that if you confess Jesus as Lord with your mouth and believe in your heart that God raised Him from the dead, you will be saved. You can yield your life over to the Lord Jesus Christ by saying this simple prayer:

Lord Jesus, I acknowledge that I'm a sinner. I believe that you came to the earth to die for my sins and you rose from the dead to give me life abundantly. I confess you as Lord of my life. I ask you to come into my heart and make me a brand new person. Amen.

If you just prayed this prayer and you meant it, Jesus has come into your life and has made you a brand new person. He has delivered you from the authority of the devil, and has given you dynamic power to live life abundantly. We will like to know of your decision, so that we can stand with you in prayer, and send you faith-building materials to help you in your walk with God.

Please write me at info@thecitylight.org or call our number toll -free: 1-888-LIGHT-21.

Endnotes

1. Loren Cunningham , Making Jesus Lord: The Dynamic Power of Laying Down Your Rights (Seattle: YWAM Publishing, 1989)

2. Rick Warren, The Purpose Driven Life: What on Earth Am I Here For? (Pennsylvania: Running Press, 2003)

3. J. Hudson Taylor, The autobiography of a man who brought the gospel to China (Bethany House, 1987)

4. Oswald J. Smith, The Man God Uses (New York: Christian Alliance Pub. Co., 1925)

5. Betty Barnett, Friend Raising (Seattle: YWAM Publishing, 2002)

6. http://www.sermoncentral.com/print_friendly.asp?Contributor ID=&sermonID=113823)

7. http://www.headstonesandmemorials.com/Epitaphs_E pitaph_Examples.php

To order more copies of this book or
other inspiring books visit:

www.thecitylight.org

More Books by the Author

1. Just Before You Say I Do: A Roadmap for Singles
2. Mission: Possible: Finding and Fulfilling your Life's Assignment
3. The Five Tests of Faith
4. Identity in Christ: Knowing The Better You and What You Can Do Through Christ
5. The 31 Immutable Laws of Relationships: Follow Them, Win Friends and Influence People
6. Live Long and Well: God's Plans for Longevity
7. Beginning With God Devotionals Series
8. Total-Life Transformation

The CityLight Publications Vision

Proclaiming and spreading

The life-changing truth of the Gospel

Through Spirit-inspired literature;

Introducing Jesus to a needy world,

Bringing life-changing revelations to Christians;

Empowering them to live their best lives n